WORLD'S GREATEST SOCCER PLAYERS

Today's Hottest Superstars

J. Alexander Poulton

OVER
TIME
BOOKS

The Publisher: Overtime Books is an imprint of Éditions de la Montagne Verte

Library and Archives Canada Cataloguing in Publication

Poulton, J. Alexander (Jay Alexander), 1977–
   The world's best soccer players: today's hottest superstars / J. Alexander Poulton.

   Includes bibliographical references.
   ISBN 13: 978-0-9737681-9-0
   ISBN 10: 0-9737681-9-3

   1. Soccer players—Biography. I. Title.

GV942.7.A1P68 2006   796.334'092'2   C2006-900268-1

Project Director: J. Alexander Poulton

Project Editors: Robert Wiznura & Virginia Gillese

Production: Willa Kung, HR Media

Cover & Title Page Images: David Beckham. Courtesy Getty Images, photograph by Denis Doyle

PC:P5

Dedication
To my brother Craig

Table of Contents

Introduction

North America has finally caught on to a sport that has attained the level of a religion in most countries around the world. With a pool of talented athletes who continually astound fans across the globe, it was only a matter of time before North America became aware of the biggest sport in the world. Soccer (football to the rest of the world) is the most widely played sport and continues to grow each year, bringing new legions of fans to support their favorite teams, from local town rivals to international champions.

Soccer athletes still have not reached the stardom of a Michael Jordan or Derek Jeter in North America, but players such as David Beckham, Ronaldinho, Zinedine Zidane, and Raul have attained a level of notoriety that surpasses their athleticism and has turned them into a new type of celebrity.

Fans follow them both on and off the field; everything from love lives to new haircuts are scrutinized under the microscopes of the press and television. However, take away all the glitz and glamour and we find some of the most talented athletes in the world performing feats of strength and delicate control not seen in any other sport.

Players like Zinedine Zidane, with his talent and sheer creativity on the field, continue to win over new fans and dazzle the old with some of the most beautiful goals ever scored in the game. During the Union of European Football Associations (UEFA) Champions League finals—a tournament held among the best teams from all participating countries—Zidane's Real Madrid was in a 1–1 tie with Bayer Leverkussen when Zidane received a long, arcing, innocent-looking pass from team-mate Roberto Carlos. Instead of putting the ball on the ground and playing it with his feet, Zidane pivoted on one foot and, before the ball had a chance to touch the field, did a karate-like kick that sent the ball sailing by some defenders and the keeper for the game-winning goal. The kick is still replayed on sports shows as one the greatest goals ever in soccer.

As with every other sport, there seems to be one country that fully embraces the culture and athleticism of the game, like Americans do with baseball and Canadians do with hockey. With soccer, the international representatives are without a doubt the Brazilians. New Brazilian stars are set to take their place alongside Pele in Brazil's continued international domination of the game with its seemingly unending supply of quality players like Ronaldinho, Kaka, Ronaldo, and Robinho. They are part of the new generation of Brazilians who have led the country to their fifth World Cup in 2002 in Korea/Japan and are the pre-tournament favorites for the 2006 World Cup in Germany.

Led by the skills of Ronaldinho, 2004 Fédération Internationale de Football Associations (FIFA) World Footballer of the Year and 2005 FIFPro player of the year, Barcelona and the Brazilian national team continue to dominate every game they play. Backing up Ronaldinho in the Brazilian midfield is one of the best players to play his position in the game today—Kaka. Strange name aside, his amazing vision of the field and pure athletic strength on the ball make him one of the most dangerous two-way players on the field. He can score a goal with the skill of Ronaldinho and make a precision pass like David Beckham. With all the young talent coming from Brazil, the future looks promising for the next World Cup.

Alongside the more seasoned players such as Zidane and Beckham, a new generation of player is making waves on both national and international scenes. Players like England's Wayne Rooney, with his explosive debut for the national team, has renewed the faith of many English fans in their homegrown talent after many years of disappointment in international competition. Portugal's Cristiano Ronaldo, another Manchester United acquisition, has astounded fans with his unique running style and amazing athleticism. Brazil's Robinho, whose dance-like dribbling techniques and scoring prowess have been compared to the legendary Pele, is making huge strides with his new team Real Madrid. Pele himself said, after seeing Robinho play, that he reminded Pele of himself when he was just breaking into the soccer world. With Rooney's strength, Ronaldo's swift feet and Robinho's creativity, there are plenty of surprises left for the next generation of soccer fans.

Soccer is also making inroads into the non-traditional major sports markets of Asia and Africa. The 2002 World Cup in Korea and Japan opened up the east as a potential pool for quality players, a pool that has never before been exploited. The world's eyes have also recently been opened up to African nations like Cameroon and Nigeria, who have stunned many with inspired underdog performances in major international competitions such as the World Cup and the Olympics.

Players such as the Republic of Korea's Ji-Sung Park or Nigeria's Jay-Jay Okocha are making names for themselves with their professional clubs and on their national teams. Korea's miraculous run in the 2002 World Cup to the semifinals was a complete surprise to the world, especially when Korea defeated such powerhouse teams as Portugal, Spain and Italy. After the World Cup, several Korean players were snatched up by prestigious European clubs and are now contributing to the success of these clubs. Although many African countries do not have the soccer infrastructure of the richer European countries, they have continually produced some of the highest quality players that fill the ranks of teams across Europe and the world.

A hundred years behind the rest of the world, the last continent to catch onto the soccer craze has been North America. The United States has been, without a doubt, one of the hardest markets for professional soccer to crack. With so many professional sports like baseball and (American) football deeply ingrained into their way of life, it has been difficult to attract fans to soccer. Baseball and football games have a proliferation of timeouts, games broken into quarters, innings and periods and a multitude of entertainment options to distract fans during a game, while soccer has no timeouts, one short halftime and low scoring games. But attitudes are changing and, with the forming of several professional level leagues, the word is finally starting to get out that professional soccer exists, and it can be exciting and fun to watch. As their men's team continues to improve—qualifying for the 2006 World Cup in

Germany—and with the women's team a constant threat (winning the Women's World Cup in 1999), the United States has been more successful in promoting the sport to a new generation. The remarkably young American Freddy Adu is bringing new interest to the game. He began his professional career at the age of 15 and is now making huge strides for Major League Soccer and for his team, D.C. United.

With its long winters and ingrained culture of hockey, Canada has been slower to embrace soccer, but a few players have managed to break the mold and make inroads in the professional European leagues. None has been more successful than Owen Hargreaves, who plays for Bayern Munich. The defensive-oriented midfielder has been a fixture on the German team since his early teens and has been getting better every year. Although he plays for the English national team, he will always remain a Canadian at heart.

No matter what age or social background—from the streets of the shantytowns in Rio de Janeiro to the local suburban leagues in England, all the way to biggest show on earth, the World Cup—soccer unites people because of their passion for the game and for the players. The best soccer players in the world aren't just those who score the most goals (although that does help). They are the solid defensemen who, without fail, stop an opponent's attack, goalkeepers, who fly through the air like Superman to stop the ball headed for the top corner with little regard for the ground rushing up at him with alarming speed, and midfielders who hardly score but assist on every single goal. Soccer is first and foremost a team game, but the individuals who stand out make the game one of the most exciting sports on the globe.

Note: All dollar figures are U.S. funds.

David Beckham
The Most Famous Player in the World

David Beckham attracts more attention these days as a celebrity than for his football skills, but the 30-year-old Real Madrid and England national midfielder can still bend the ball around the field to find an open teammate or the back of the opponent's net.

The England captain has lost a bit of his luster over the past few years because critics say that he has become more of a movie-star-type celebrity and less the football player that got him the attention he deserved at first. His much-photographed relationship with ex-Spice Girl Victoria Adams (Posh Spice) has been fodder for the British tabloid media since they first got wind that the young handsome English superstar playing for Manchester United was dating the glamorous pop star. As the shine from the relationship faded in the media (trips to school and lunch with his children just aren't that exciting), criticism of Beckham has shifted. Advertising has made David Beckham one of the most recognizable faces on the planet and, in recent years, it seems that Beckham has more advertising deals than goals.

Over his career, he has been on the covers of countless magazines and newspapers and has appeared in hundreds of advertisements. The paparazzi follow Beckham and his family more closely than they do the British Royal family. He has several books and even had a movie named after him (*Bend it like Beckham*). Whenever he leaves his home, he has a pack of paparazzi vehicles hounding his every move. He has become so famous that even his hairstyle garners press.

Media love to see the meteoric rise and fall of celebrity, but Beckham, through all the pressure, has kept his focus on the game. As Beckham puts it, "I've always said that I work hard at football, and I love my football. I have a hard life…well, actually, it's not that hard a life. It's a great life."

In an interview with *Striker* Magazine, Beckham says, "It's the one thing I always wanted to do. Even now, at 30 years old, I still want to get better at things. I still practice free kicks."

Despite all the criticism, Beckham's passion for the game hasn't changed. While he could not lead the English national team to victory in the 2002 World Cup or the 2004 European Championship, he turned things around in mid-season 2004–05 after a lackluster first year with Real Madrid. Playing with the other "galacticos" (Spanish word for the team of superstar players in Madrid) of Real Madrid, Beckham's footballing fortunes have shifted as he has once again found the power and accuracy to his kick that made him famous. Beckham has now silenced his many critics with some of the best football he has played in years.

Real Madrid's "galacticos" were brought to the team with the hope of bringing utter dominance of the Spanish League and, quite possibly, the UEFA Champions league. When 2003 went by with little success for the high-paid team, critics pounced on its most popular player. After all, Real Madrid had paid 40 million dollars for David Beckham with the hope that his accurate passes and legendary free kicks would spark the already stacked team to even greater heights. So when the walls came tumbling down after a poor performance in 2003, the start of the next season came with immediate expectations of failure.

The 2004 season started off the same way the previous season had ended, and Beckham was once again at the center of Real fans' expectations. Never one to back away from a challenge, Beckham answered his detractors at the season's halfway mark when shades of the old David Beckham began to appear. Back were the incredible bending free kicks that goalkeepers always seemed to have difficulty getting their hands on, let alone stopping. The patented crosses into the penalty area to team-mates Raul and Ronaldo had returned, and those perfectly executed passes that Beckham does so well were once again on target. He has done it countless times, and the story usually sounds like...

The defenders pass the ball back and forth across the pitch, as Beckham tries to position himself to receive the ball. The pass comes in hard from his teammate. Beckham takes the pass directly in the chest, and the ball somehow flutters down to where his feet are waiting to take the ball up field. He quickly surveys the pitch to spot his teammates. Through a group of defenders, Beckham spots his teammate making his way toward a less-crowded area of the box. After a few more yards, Beckham plays the ball around one defender and lets off a high shot toward the box without even looking to see if Raul is there to accept the pass. It seems like an eternity for the ball to get there. The ball floats toward the goal. A head rises from the mess of bodies and miraculously finds the back of the net. A beautiful goal, and an even more incredible pass from Beckham.

While he can never be called the complete player, throughout his career Beckham has shown moments of sheer brilliance, making him one the game's current outstanding players. Whenever he takes a free kick within striking distance of the net, opposing teams always try to creep the wall a little closer to the invisible line, trying to take away that extra bit of curving space that a Beckham shot seems to take before suddenly bending around the corner and appearing before the goaltender, who has just a fraction of a second to react before the ball goes crashing into the back of the net.

In the next few years, Beckham seeks to break new ground in his career. The 30-year-old English national captain is far from retirement age, but the idea is never far from his mind. He realizes that his time is limited when it comes to the success of the English team in international competition. The 2006 World Cup in Germany is where Beckham hopes to put to rest the debate about his skills and lead his team to the finals.

"Everyone is talking about the excitement of the World Cup coming up next summer, but we have a lot of work to do to get to the World Cup finals before we start talking about how well we can do," said Beckham in a Sky news interview.

The international stage is where the true measure of a player's skill is marked in the annals of soccer. Would Pele have been so widely regarded as the best in the world if he had never led Brazil to several World Cups? Would Maradona's skill be so widely recognized without his successes for Argentina? Or to take the opposite case, is Roberto Baggio remembered for his outstanding career or for his famous missed opportunity in the shootout in the World Cup final in 1994 against Brazil? It's a thin line for Beckham to walk, but he wants to prove to his country and to himself that he can bring glory back to the English inventors of the game.

Whether we like him or not, a player such as Beckham not only brings notoriety to any team he plays for, he also brings a determination and ability to make the plays that mean the difference between victory and defeat. Does it really matter if he looks good doing it?

Wayne Rooney
The True Street Soccer Player

When Wayne Rooney got the call at his home in the tough working-class district of Liverpool that he would be a replacement player on the Everton squad against English Premiership Champions Arsenal that night in October 2002, he did not realize that his amazing performance on the pitch would spark the start of a brilliant career at the tender age of 16. On that night, he scored the winning goal off a cannon-like shot that found the back of the net with just a minute or two remaining in the game.

The Everton fans' prayers had been answered. They had been searching for the miracle player who could bring back glory to the Everton Blues, and Rooney was their man. In just his second game with Everton, against Leeds United, fans were positively assured that the young man from Liverpool could take them to new heights when he scored the only goal of the game. The goal came on a magnificent run where Rooney passed a few defenders at the halfway line before coolly slipping the ball in from just inside the penalty area. Everton's love affair with Rooney continued for the rest of the season as fans saw a new reason for hope in the play of the young bruiser from Liverpool.

Everton manager David Moyes summed up Rooney's talent perfectly, "Wayne is a football person. He hasn't been brought up on all the comforts that are associated with the modern academy player. He has been brought up the old-fashioned way, and you can tell with that spirit and, well, devilment that he's got. He's a street footballer, and that's why we like him so much."

Success continued for Rooney when he joined the national team to play his first international game against Australia at the age of just 17 years and 111 days. He set the record for England's youngest player ever to score on the international stage when he scored the winning goal during a game against Macedonia. While his success piled up on the international stage, his time with Everton was slipping away. Despite the fans' loyal support for their new local hero, Everton as a team just wasn't winning games and, as Everton's fortunes fell, Rooney looked elsewhere to find his football glory.

"It was a tough decision to leave Everton, the club I've supported and played for all my life, but

I am excited to be joining a club as big as Manchester United," said Rooney after the trade.

The elite teams with all the money can smell talent a mile away, and it wasn't long before Manchester United came knocking with a fat contract in hand. The contract to obtain Rooney calls for Manchester to pay $33 million, with most of the money going to Everton. The 17-year-old Rooney was at the top of soccer world now that he had a place on one of the most revered teams in soccer history, and the fresh-faced kid could do no wrong.

His first game in Manchester United colors, against Fenerbahce of Turkey in UEFA Champions league play, was one to remember and made Rooney an instant star with the extremely demanding United fans. In a game that was dominated by Manchester, Rooney led the way with three spectacular goals, trouncing the overwhelmed Turkish side 6–2. Rooney proved in one game that Manchester got what they had paid for, and he was just getting started.

Rooney showed in that one game that he could not only be in the right place at the right time to score goals, but that he could also create the space needed for opportunities and score the kind of goals to make him into one of the best players in the game. It is this potential that frightens Rooney's opponents.

"I like the sort of striker who will score all on his own if he wants to, and Rooney showed again the other night that he is capable of doing that. He can shoot from distance, get on the end of crosses, hit free kicks—anything. He's not the same type of finisher as Michael Owen or Ruud van Nistelrooy, but he is definitely the sort of player I would pay to watch," said Arsenal striker Thierry Henry of his young opponent. "He is someone who plays with absolutely no fear, and when you have a striker like that then there are no limits. English football is very fortunate to have such a great striker,"

Rooney is the sort of player that cannot be made by any special training. He was born with the talent and physical attributes that make him one of the best in the game today at such a young age. His instincts on the field are what matter the most and what will bring him to the level that he can achieve. But, occasionally, other things get in the way.

As Rooney quickly learns the skills to succeed on the field, the fame and celebrity that come with the success have taken their toll on the street-baller from Liverpool. Not used to the media attention and scrutiny that comes with success, Rooney has had encounters with the media that have been less than pleasant. It might not sound like much to North American audiences familiar with the misdeeds of sports stars, but when he showed up at the BBC sports awards and accepted his award for Young Sports Personality of the Year chewing gum and leaving the top button of his shirt undone, he was promptly railed in the British press for his lack of respect. Rooney was also excluded from attending an awards banquet because of his reputation for expressing himself with words of the "four-letter" variety both on and off the football field.

Even though Rooney now makes close to $90,000 a week, he still remains the tough kid from the streets of Liverpool, but don't expect his coach to change a thing. Rooney admits, "If you believe all the things written about you when you're doing well you have to look at them when you are not having the same success. You only need one bad game, and things change and that can knock your confidence if you let it. It can all become too much if you let yourself get carried away by it." He adds, "I see all the stuff written in the papers and know it's a talking point. But this side of my temperament is a big part of my game. If there is a tackle to be won I'm going to go in for it—even if it means getting booked. I'm not going to pull out of tackles because I'm worried about picking up a yellow card."

At 19-years of age, Rooney has the ability that Zinedine Zidane, Roberto Baggio and Maradonna had when they were his age. The final test for the young striker will be getting to that level of excellence, and Rooney, along the way, plans to have as much fun as possible.

Frank Lampard
Better with Age

The pressure weighed heavily on Frank Lampard's shoulders even before he made his first professional appearance for West Ham United. As the son of assistant coach Frank Lampard Sr. and the nephew of manager Harry Redknapp, the media and fans believed that Frank Jr. was on the team only because of family connections and not because he earned his spot as the others players had.

In the beginning, the fans had reason to doubt Lampard's position on the team because, for the first year or two, he had trouble finding his place and wasn't producing the goals or assists expected of him. He also earned the unfortunate nickname of "Fat Frank" because of his...sturdy frame. After losing a few pounds, Lampard soon found his pace on the field and, by his third year with West Ham, had turned things around and finally won over the skeptical fans.

With his family at his side, Lampard improved his skills every year, but he knew that he wasn't being challenged in his game by the coach and other players on his team. He knew that if he didn't change teams he might never improve as he wanted, so he began to look around the league for another team that would meet his needs.

Lampard's decision was made easier when his father and uncle were fired from the team, and he quickly made known that he wanted a transfer out of West Ham United. After some speculation about which team he would sign with, the midfielder found a home with Chelsea at the cost of $16 million. Although his first two years with the team were shaky, given the outstanding play of teammate and midfielder Gianfranco Zola (who started most games ahead of the new recruit), Lampard finally got his chance to prove himself when Zola was traded.

Despite the slow start, Lampard adapted to Chelsea's style of play and improved his game. By the 2003–04 season, Lampard was a fixture on Chelsea's midfield, starting in every game of the Premiership season, a fact almost unheard of in a league rife with talent and coaches known for constantly changing the lineup to match individual opponents.

Lampard slowly evolved into a prolific goal scorer for a midfield player. His hefty frame doesn't allow him to have the same pace of a midfielder like Pavel Nedved, but once he is on stride, he is difficult to stop because of his strength. Lampard can shoot with equal power from both his left and right foot, and this skill, combined with his excellent vision on the field, makes him a deadly opponent in or near the penalty area. On the defensive side, his large frame comes in handy in blocking the opposing midfielders from crossing the ball to their strikers, and he isn't afraid to finish on a challenge when required. Wrap all these talents up into a player that consistently performs at a high level, and you have a player that is an indispensable asset to his team.

Under coach Claudio Ranieri, Chelsea was a good team, but the players still lacked a certain confidence when it came to playing against stronger teams such as Manchester United and Arsenal. When Jose Mourinho joined Chelsea as their new head coach, his confidence and ability to motivate players was a welcome change from the more timid Ranieri.

"The most important change is that the mental attitude now is: win, win, win. At times it wasn't like that last season. Now the accent is on winning every game we play—and every competition we're in," said Lampard, regarding the arrival of Mourinho as head coach.

The feeling was mutual for Mourinho, who was already a Lampard supporter before arriving at Chelsea. "I love Lampard, and you can write that," Mourinho told reporters. "I want to change Frank as a player, I want to make him a better one. With the team's help, he can be the best."

Unlike coach Ranieri, Mourinho focused the players' training on drills that could be used in game situations. With Ranieri, the Chelsea players had felt they had to perform on the fly, which left them running around without a system in place against the more difficult teams like Arsenal. With Mourinho, the players worked a lot harder in practice and on the field, but they never once complained about his tactics because they knew that each move he made was pre-planned and well thought.

"In the build-up to the game, the manager will have prepared us for every possibility. He'll say, 'If this happens, we might change to this.' It's never off-the-cuff as it was under Ranieri. It's always something that has been pre-planned," said Lampard in an interview with the *Times*.

Mourinho knew that Lampard possessed all the skills he would need to become a great player, but to bring his game to a higher level, he had to improve his mental game as much as his physical. Only these changes would allow him enough improvement to secure his place in the soccer history books. Lampard did his part by staying long after practices were over, working on his conditioning and ball-handling skills. He began to improve immediately. This drive to succeed under pressure makes Lampard one of the best at his position.

With a renewed confidence in his game, Lampard was the key ingredient in Chelsea's run to the Barclay's English Premiership title with a remark-able 29 wins, 8 draws and 1 loss. He scored a career high of 13 goals and was one of the best players on the field in the Champions League. Unfortu-nately, Premier League rival Liverpool took Chelsea out of Champions League in the semifinals, and

Lampard did not get the chance to raise the Cup above his head.

"It was a terrible night with bad memories for everybody," recalled John Terry, Chelsea captain and star defender.

Lampard's skills were not overlooked for the national team, having had early success with the under-21 team. He had a total of 19 appearances, and he captained most of the games. Despite this success, he was left out of full international competition in the 2000 European Cup and the 2002 World Cup finals, despite having a good season with Chelsea. He finally got the recognition from England coach Sven Goran Eriksson for the 2004 Euro Cup in Portugal, and Lampard was placed on the first team for the elimination rounds. He proved a wise addition when he scored England's only goal in a match against France and used his defensive skills to keep each game as close as possible.

"Now I feel I'm part of the team and expect to be starting. That's what I always wanted," said Lampard.

Despite a team that consists of players like Wayne Rooney, David Beckham and Steven Gerrard, England has failed to make a significant showing on the international level. Lampard is the first to admit his failings when it comes to his performance for his country.

In the 2006 World Cup qualifying rounds, Lampard admitted that the criticism leveled at him from coach Eriksson was completely justified. "When Sven said about me not being on top form, I think he is right. It is early in the season and it would be strange to be on top form now and to try and keep that up all season," said Lampard in an interview with sportinglife.com. "I don't think Sven was criticizing me, he made a fair statement. I think he could have made it about anyone in the team at this stage of the season because not too many are firing on all cylinders."

A lot of pressure is on the English side this year as they have one of the best teams on paper that they have had in a number of years. Again, Lampard remains cool under pressure and foresees the squad living up to the expectations of the nation.

"If I was on top form now I would be worried that I could sustain it all season, including the important part of the season and the World Cup itself, so hopefully I will keep building up and surpass what I did last year," said Lampard.

He has come a long way from the "Fat Frank" moniker he earned in his days in West Ham United to the Premiership with Chelsea, but he still has many mountains to climb. He wants to prove himself in international competition, and with Chelsea, hopefully in another run to the Champions League title. If he continues to improve the way he has over the past few years, then the sky is the limit for this versatile midfielder.

Zinedine Zidane
He Who Stands Alone

Born in the poorest part of the French city of Marseilles to an Algerian father and a French mother far away from the sun and sand of the tourist areas, Zidane sought refuge from the crime of the streets at the local football field. The Zidanes did not have much money, so young Zinedine spent most of his time at the field, which was set between a government building and a fountain. Over and over again, he practiced all the tricks and moves that would later earn him the FIFA World Footballer of the Year Award three times.

The talents of the young Frenchman were noted early on in his life, and by the time he was 18 he had signed with his first professional team for the French Division One football club in Cannes in 1988. It wasn't until two seasons later that he was regularly appearing in club matches and scored his first goal against Nantes in a 2–1 victory. However, the soccer world didn't discover Zidane's talents

until his trade to Bordeaux where he became one
of the most sought-after players in Europe.

In his first year with the club, Zidane found a team
and league that were more on par with his style
of play, and he quickly doubled his previous season
high of 5 goals to 10. The defining moment of his
time with Bordeaux came when the team made it
to the quarterfinals in the UEFA Cup and faced
off against AC Milan, one of the most difficult
teams to beat at the time. Although they lost in
the first leg of the quarterfinals, it was the second
leg comeback that caught everyone's attention
and taught Zidane a valuable lesson in his professional career.

"This was my first great victory, my first incredible win," said Zidane in a *Soccer Digest* interview.
"Obviously people would argue that the World
Cup final against Brazil and my two goals that day
was the greatest moment in my career. This game
had a huge impact on the rest of my career
because I learned how to win that night—I tasted
victory for the first time."

Although Bordeaux went on to beat Slavia
Prague in the semifinals, they lost to Bayern
Munich in the finals. Zidane had learned what it
took to win at the highest of the professional levels
and that knowledge would serve him well when
he made his next move up the soccer ladder to the
Italian Serie A league with his new team, Juventus.
French soccer legend Michel Platini told the Italian

team, "With Zidane, you'll have it all—vision, ball control, class."

With Juventus, Zidane honed the skills that make him the greatest player in soccer today. In his first year, Zidane helped the team to the Serie A title two years running as well as UEFA Champions League final, unfortunately losing both Champ finals. The sense of loss at the Champions finals did not last long because Zidane led his country through to the World Cup finals for the first time.

Although the 1998 FIFA World Cup was held in France, nobody expected that the host country would win the Cup let alone make it through to the final. But under the captainship of Zinedine Zidane all seemed possible for Les Bleus.

The road to the final wasn't a smooth one for Zidane and the French side. After a close victory against Paraguay at 113 minutes into extra time, they came close to losing to a strong Italian team in a shootout in the quarterfinals. But France prevailed when Italian Luigi Di Biagio missed the final shot, giving the French a 4–3 win on penalties. After beating Croatia 2–1 in the semifinals, it was on to the finals against Brazil, where Zidane took center stage and assured his place in the history of soccer.

Zidane woke that morning on July 12, 1998, knowing that he was about to play the biggest game of his life. The 75,000 fans at the Stade de France were working themselves into a frenzy before the start of the game. As the players walked out onto the field, the full force of the moment hit them.

"I didn't realize what was happening to me. And then, from that moment on, time flew," said Zidane reflecting back on the moments before the start of the match.

The French, led by captain Zidane, quickly established the pace of the match-up. The normally swift-footed Brazilians looked sluggish around the French as Zidane put France on the scoreboard with a brilliant header at the 27-minute mark of the first half. Not known for using his head often, Zidane made a beautiful jump in the air past the Brazilian defenders and headed the ball strongly past the keeper.

As the halfway mark approached, Zidane rushed into the penalty area and jumped through the crowd to catch another header and put the French up by two goals going into the second half. The huge crowd at the metropolitan Paris Stadium was chanting his name over and over again. France had a new hero. Emmanuel Petit put the game away at the 90-minute mark with a third goal, and France erupted with joy with the final whistle. They'd won the country's first ever World Cup title.

As the parade erupted from the stadium onto Paris streets, thousands gathered around the Arc de Triomphe where a huge projection of Zidane's face was pasted with the words "Zidane for President" underneath the picture. To make his year even more special, Zidane won the FIFA World Footballer of the Year award for his outstanding play in club and international competition. He spent three more years with Juventus, won another championship title for his country at the 2000 European Cup and collected his second World Footballer of the Year Award.

Although he had been incredibly successful with Juventus, Zidane was still missing the one trophy that he most wanted. Juventus had a good team, but Zidane felt that with a team in the Spanish League he would have a better chance at getting a hold of the one trophy that had eluded him several times in his career—the UEFA Champions League title. The first team he looked to join was Spanish Liga's perennial favorites Real Madrid.

The deal that sent Zidane from Juventus to Real Madrid was the highest price ever paid for an athlete in any sport: $64.6 million. Real Madrid was building a team of superstars, and Zidane was the ultimate edition to the "galacticos" squad. He joined the ranks of Raul, Roberto Carlos, Ronaldo, and Beckham to make Real Madrid the highest-paid team in sports. A lot of expectations were placed on the superstar team, and when Zidane did not live up to people's expectations of what a player of his caliber could achieve, fans began to question whether the owner had received the bad end of the most expensive deal in sports.

But Zidane's slight slump would never have been questioned had he been just any other player. His skills were no longer doubted when Real Madrid made it to the Champions League final against Germany's Bayer Leverkusen. Zidane scored one of the most beautiful goals in the history of the game.

With the game deadlocked at 1–1, it seemed destined to go into the dreaded shootouts to decide the winner. Both teams appeared content to play a defensive match, not wanting to make any mistakes that would give the game to the other team. Everything was going according to plan for the Leverkusen players as Real Madrid carried another attack into their zone. The Bayer defense held the Madrid strikers to the outside of the penalty area and were waiting for the easy shot to come in so they could start their run into Madrid's zone. But Zidane had something different in mind on this rush.

The goal came on the most innocent-looking of plays. The Leverkusen players thought the play was just another simple pass to Zidane. However, Zidane had a clear line to the net and decided to take the Roberto Carlos cross on the volley rather than chesting it down to make the play in two touches. The ball seem to float in the air as it headed for Zidane who pivoted on one foot and swung his free leg as if he was doing a move from a kung fu movie, and he connected perfectly with the ball. The ball sailed past the stunned Leverkusen defenders and goalkeeper and into the back of the net. He put his team ahead with one of the most spectacular goals ever scored and made legions of new fans. The chants of Zidane for president only got louder after that goal.

Although he would receive another FIFA World Footballer of the Year trophy in 2003, success eluded Zidane once again on the international scene after France's disappointing results at the Euro Cup 2004. At this time, he decided to retire from international soccer altogether and focus his career on league play. Since their victory in the Champions league final in 2000, Real Madrid have failed to live up to the "galacticos" brand, and they have found themselves struggling to keep up with teams like Barcelona. But recently, when news spread that key players like Claude Makalele and Thierry Henry would be playing for France in Germany, Zidane came back from his international retirement. With all he has accomplished, Zidane wants one more shot at the top of the world. Allez Zizou!

Thierry Henry
The Constant Successes

To see Thierry Henry play soccer is to watch a master creating artwork. He is the perfect athlete in every sense of the word. His ball-handling skills are something to behold; he once bounced the ball down the field for several yards on his knees and feet without the ball touching the ground, all the while avoiding the defenders desperately trying to get the ball from him. He is an aggressive competitor on the field, often getting into heated discussions with referees, coaches, teammates and even with himself when he does not perform to the highest of standards. Thierry Henry is an asset to any team lucky enough to have him.

The team lucky enough to have Henry now, Arsenal of the English Premier League, is currently reaping the benefits of the 28-year-old French striker's talents. However, when he began his professional career with Monaco in 1994, he wasn't yet the phenomenon that had him named runner up, two years in a row, as FIFA World Footballer of the Year.

For his first two years, Henry was used sparingly by the Monaco coach in favor of the older, more experienced players. But soon Henry's talents were too good to go unused, and by his third season with Monaco, he was a team regular, playing over 30 regular season games. However, he still had not achieved the success he was looking for and that he knew he could attain. After an excellent performance for France during their 1998 run to the World Cup, Henry knew he could be a player like Zidane, a player that a franchise could build a team around. After two lackluster seasons, one more with Monaco and one with Juventus Turin, Henry found his way to the Arsenal Football Club.

Most players entering the English Premier League need time to adjust to the different style of play than that of the mainland European leagues, but Henry made his presence felt immediately, with his best season to date, and earned himself a new legion of fans.

Arsenal and Henry are a match made in heaven. In his first year with the team, he scored 17 goals in 31 games and led the team into the UEFA Cup finals, only to lose to Turkish Galatasaray. The UEFA Cup loss was quickly put out of his mind, however, as France continued its domination on the international circuit with a win at the 2000 European Championship. And things just kept getting better for Henry.

In 2002, Arsenal dominated the English Premier League, winning the regular season title and the Football Association (FA) Cup. Henry, meanwhile, picked up the Premiership top-scorer award with 24 goals in 31 games. After another successful year and a repeat win of the FA Cup, fans and media almost began to expect the French striker and his Arsenal team to win all the time. Amazingly enough, Henry and Arsenal didn't disappoint their fans, for they lost not a game in the Premiership league, a feat that has only been accomplished more than a century ago in the late 1800s. But the problem of perfection is that there is nowhere to go, and Henry felt pressured to produce.

"The expectations of people for us after the season we had last year were so high," said Henry in an interview with *Striker* magazine. "There is two parts to it. I would never say that we had an okay season. I would always say that we expected to do better. Even when we went unbeaten in the league last year, I thought we could have done better in the Champions League and the FA Cup. That is always my mentality."

As the new 2005–06 season got under way, Henry started off with a bit of bad luck by injuring himself during a game he was playing for France in the qualifying rounds for the 2006 World Cup. The injury put a dent into his desire to overtake Arsenal's record for the most club goals. The record was set by legendary Arsenal striker Ian Wright at 185 goals, but Henry, with an injury that won't keep him out for long, will break that record and is likely to go on to set some records of his own.

Djibril Cisse
The New Breed

His look is unmistakable. The dark skin, heavily contrasted with the ever-changing bleach-blonde hair, and the set of glaring eyes that shake the nerve of any defenders facing him on the field make Dijbril Cisse one of the most recognizable faces on the field. Add to that intimidating look his incredible speed and athleticism and you have the complete soccer player in Djibril Cisse, French national and Liverpool striker.

As the youngest of seven children brought up by a single mother, Cisse was raised in the French town of Arles, where he learned from an early age that soccer was his one true passion and outlet because he couldn't afford much else. The practice of his childhood paid off for Cisse; he is one of the fastest strikers in the game today.

However, Cisse wasn't always the sought-after player that he is today. When he made his professional debut with the French club Auxerre, he played the first two seasons on the sidelines before getting the nod regularly in league play. His breakout year came in the 2000–01 season when Auxerre striker Stephane Guivarc'h was sidelined with an injury, and coach Guy Roux was forced to use Cisse for the remainder of the season. Roux, not one to change his way of thinking easily, reluctantly replaced Guivarc'h with Cisse, and got immediate results as Cisse scored eight goals in 25 games. Roux needed even less convincing to keep Cisse when he scored four goals against Rennes during the first game of the 2001–02 season and finally finished the season with an amazing 22 goals in 29 games. The next two seasons with Auxerre would be known as the Cisse years.

Blessed with incredible speed and the ability to shoot with equal power from both legs, Cisse became the player to go to when goals were needed. After three seasons, playing in 100 games, Cisse had scored 62 league goals and was the colorful favorite of the Auxerre fans. But the romance wouldn't last long because Cisse wanted a change of scenery and a new set of challenges to a game that had become a little predictable with an Auxerre squad heavily reliant on his talents. Cisse quickly found a new home with the Liverpool Football Club of the English Premier League. But the transition wasn't as smooth as he would have liked.

"At first, I admit it was difficult," said Cisse in an interview with *FourFourTwo* magazine. "Most foreign players need a bit of time to adapt when they arrive in England. I can take criticism, all the time it's fair. People pay their money to come to the stadium, and they expect you to give your best."

Even though he scored in his first match with Liverpool against the Tottenham HotSpurs, not all were convinced that Cisse was worth the money they spent on attaining him from Auxerre. Local British papers editorialized and picked apart Cisse in all aspects of his game, from his commitment to the team to his occasional lukewarm performances on the field. It got even worse for Cisse when he broke his leg in an incident with Blackburn Rover's defender Jamie McEveley.

As Cisse came sprinting at full speed trying to get around McEveley, the two went down awkwardly near the goal. The resulting scream that came from Cisse silenced the capacity crowd, who looked on in horror at his shinbone protruding from the sock covering his lower leg. Doctors said he was finished for the season at best, given the extent of his break. Cisse preferred to look at things a little differently.

"When I look back on it now, I have to say that despite my injury, it was the greatest season of my career," said Cisse.

Defying all expectations, Cisse made a brief appearance in the Champions League quarterfinal match against Juventus and made his full return in the final match in the English Premiership against Aston Villa, scoring two goals. Cisse credits the support staff at Liverpool for nursing him back to health, and he credits the time off he had with allowing him to train and improve his fitness, thus bringing him into better shape than he was before the injury. He came back to the field just in time to join his teammates as they went into the Champions final against the mighty AC Milan.

Nobody picked Liverpool to make it to the finals, and no one predicted that they could challenge, let alone beat, the strong Italian team. So it wasn't surprising to any observers that AC Milan went up 3 goals to none early in the game. Cisse was still on the bench, his hopes sinking lower and lower as time passed by without the Liverpool strikers breaking the defensive zone of AC Milan.

However, as quickly as AC Milan had scored their three goals, Liverpool answered back with three goals of their own from Steven Gerrard, Vladimir Smicer and Xabi Alonso. Replacing Liverpool striker Milan Baros in the 85th minute, Cisse looked nervous and hesitant on the ball, not the way he wanted to cap off his triumphant return. Luckily, the game ended after extra time with the score tied, forcing a shoot out. With Liverpool already ahead in the shootout, Cisse stepped up to the penalty spot to take his shot. With the noise from the thousands of Liverpool fans at the stadium in Istanbul echoing in his ears, Cisse tapped the ball into the lower corner of the net confidently as Milan keeper Dida guessed the wrong direction of the shot and missed the save. Liverpool held on to their lead, and when Liverpool keeper Jerzy Dudek stopped the final shot, his teammates rushed across the field in triumph.

"I remember going mad during the huge celebrations. I was in a trance," recalled Cisse. "Unforgettable. Crazy. Amazing. A night to remember, to cherish."

Cisse's next challenge is to prove to his critics that he can be a top goal scorer in the English league and not just a one hit wonder. His lavish wedding to his English bride Jude Littler was fodder for the tabloids, proof that he has become of interest both for what he does on the field and off. But it's on the field where he has most to lose and everything to gain. Not one for modesty, Cisse has predicted his own success and the success of his team in the Premiership standings: "People are going to see another Djibril Cisse—this is my season."

Paolo Maldini
AC Milan's Reliable Old Man

A fixture on the AC Milan defense since he started with the team in January 1985 against Udinese at the age of 16, Paolo Maldini was a fan favorite even before he started. For the past 50 years of AC Milan history, there has been a Maldini on the team. Five years before Paolo was born, his father Cesare ran the ball for Milan when they won their first European Championship Cup in 1963. To say that the game of soccer is in his blood would be an understatement: he was born to play. He quickly emerged from his father's shadow to become a great player for Milan and the Italian national team.

For the past two decades, Maldini has been the heart and soul of the Milan defensive core. His coolness on the field and the way he effortlessly protects the keeper have kept the club at the top of the Italian Serie A division for years and made it always a major contender in the inter-league games. Although Maldini has spent two successful decades on defense, when he first started in soccer he wanted to be put on midfield because no one ever scores goals on defense but rather is blamed for the ones that are scored on their team. Luckily, Maldini was steered in the right direction and chose the harder path. He can score a goal just like other players, but his excellent vision of the field and ability to foresee where the ball will go (so that he can strip it from the striker) makes him perfectly suited for his position.

He makes defending look easy out on the field so that opponents often underestimate him on their attack, though they quickly learn that the elder statesman of Italian soccer still has a few tricks up his sleeve. He hardly ever commits a foul, and on occasion, after stripping the striker of a ball, he likes to venture in on attacks—if the play and score permit him to take the chance.

Maldini, however, is not the perfect player—he often lacks speed on an opponent's rushes, and he has made glaring errors in big games. His giveaway goal to a Korean player in the 2002 World Cup, for example, came from a moment of inattention, forcing Italy from the competition. While he has disappointed internationally, he more than makes up for his faults in his role as a teacher to the other defenders like Jaap Stam, Cafu, and Alessandro Nesta on his AC Milan squad. They have all benefited from his two decades of experience.

"I admire many things about Maldini, starting with his immense class, which has made him one of the best and most complete defenders in football," said legendary Italian goalkeeper and former national team coach Dino Zoff, "but also his professionalism, great preparation and commitment for both his club and the national team."

Maldini recently surpassed Dino Zoff's record 570th Serie A appearance in the AC Milan uniform, thus ensuring the 37-year-old a place in the Italian soccer record books. In his many appearances with Milan, Maldini has won seven Serie A titles, four European Champions League Cups, four UEFA Super Cups, One Coppa Italia, four Italian Super Cups and two European/South American Cups. He nearly added another Champions League title in 2005 but lost on penalties in a heartbreaker to Liverpool.

When playing for his country, Maldini has put in the same amount of effort as he has elsewhere, but he has consistently come up short in his search for soccer's biggest prizes. His first chance at the World Cup was when Italy hosted the tournament in 1990. The Azzuri (Italian nickname for the national team) only finished in third place when they lost to Argentina on penalties in the semi-finals. Four years later, Italy and Maldini once again felt the sting of a game decided on penalties when they lost to Brazil off the famous Roberto Baggio missed penalty. That moment would be the closest Maldini came to holding the golden trophy. Another disappointing loss happened in 1998 against France in the quarterfinals, yet again on penalties and another in 2002, when World Cup host Korea took them out of the tournament. After 2002, Maldini decided to retire from international football to let some of the younger guys have a chance at the World Cup and to focus solely on his career with AC Milan. It was a sad way to leave the international competitions, but Maldini's mark will not be forgotten. His native country put on a very public campaign in the weeks leading up to the 2004 Euro Cup in Portugal for him to come out of international retirement and captain the team in one last effort to win a title. He declined for personal reasons.

Things continue to go well for Maldini, however, with AC Milan. Although the team lost to Liverpool in the Champions League final, it was Maldini who opened the scoring in the game with a record-setting goal just 51 seconds into the start of the first half.

"I still get goosebumps when I recall that double save from Shevchenko," said Maldini, referring to the save by Liverpool keeper Jerzy Dudek on Milan's Andriy Shevchenko in the penalty shootout.

Victory wasn't meant to be that night in Istanbul, but Maldini still has some fight left in him. He has recently signed on for another two years with Milan. At 37, he doesn't seem to be slowing down.

Francesco Totti
Italian Bad Boy

All the scouting reports on Francesco Totti say that he is one of the best power strikers with a fine touch on the ball, but that he never has developed his potential because of constant problems with management, other players, himself and, seemingly always, with the media.

His skill is obvious when he is having a good game. Totti's amazing athleticism and goal-scoring prowess have earned him a legion of fans in Italy and the Roma Football Club. Just as Brazilian soccer has developed a reputation for offensive-minded play with a focus on individual talent, Italian soccer has become known for its defensive play with the focus on team defense. Totti did not fit well into the typical Italian defensive mold. He possesses incredible handling skills and is able to split the defense and take a shot with both his right and left leg with equal power. This diversity allows the coach to use Totti almost anywhere on the field. He can be placed at midfield and use his excellent vision of the field to make key passes, and he can also be relied upon to make key defensive saves on opposition rushes.

A rarity in all sports, Totti started his career with the team he supported as a boy and will probably end his career with—Serie A Club AS Roma. In his early years with the club, Totti flourished with Roma and earned full player status in his sophomore season with 4 goals in 21 games. Totti credits the development of his skills to coach Zdenek Zeman, who trained him to focus on his natural talents as a striker rather than becoming simply a well-rounded player. Zeman wanted Totti to be a threat every time he got the ball between his feet.

A skilled player is judged by his performance on the field; a great player is judged by his performance on an international stage. Like Beckham, Totti must elevate his game when it comes to international competition as did the greats like Pele, Maradona, Ronaldo and many others. They all played well on their regular local teams but stepped up their games come crunch time. The world never would have heard of the amazing exploits of these two players if they had never led their teams to victory on the international stage. The players would have stayed simple, local heroes, wherever they played. Questions of ability continue to linger over Totti's career, for he has never stepped beyond the confines of his career with AS Roma, and his performances with the Italian national team have been less than inspiring at times.

The 2004 European Cup was a proving ground for Totti after a less than spectacular performance at the 2002 World Cup where he failed to live up to expectations again when he was thrown out of a game, for diving, against South Korea. Although the judgment was considered a little harsh, Totti let his emotions get the better of him. Italy eventually lost the match and was eliminated from the World Cup tournament. The most glaring example of his lackluster performances on the field came during the 2004 Euro Cup in Portugal in a game that saw Totti's Italy take on Denmark.

It was an important game for the Azzuri's, who hadn't performed to their capabilities in the lead-up to the Euro Cup game against Denmark. Totti performed well despite the team's disappointing results, but he could not seem to find his rhythm in the tournament. Denmark's Christian Poulsen was assigned to shadow Totti for the match and contain the Italian striker's fast breaks or quality passes. A television camera never took its eye off Totti and Poulsen, following the two as they battled for position on the field. Totti could not adapt to Poulsen's excellent defending and looked increasingly frustrated as the match wore on. Time after time when Totti got the ball between his feet, Poulsen would be on top of him, frustrating him each time. What happened next was caught on the camera that had been following him around for the entire game and was available for the entire world to see. The frustration was apparent on Totti's face as Poulsen yet again got the ball away from him on a tackle. You could almost predict that something was going to happen, and Totti did not disappoint. With the camera clearly focused on

Totti, and after the referee had blown the play dead, Totti walked by Poulsen and spat directly in his face, following this insult with a volley of curse words. Poulsen pulled his head back in disgust and went directly to the referee. Totti was thrown out of the game and given a three-game suspension for his disgusting gesture.

"We will not tolerate this kind of behavior," said UEFA spokesman William Gaillard in response to the Totti incident. "We did not tolerate it in the past, and we will not tolerate it in the future."

Italian media love a good scandal, and Totti was not spared after this incident. Totti was smashed in the media for abandoning the national team, and his temper became the butt of many jokes. His antics had landed him into trouble before, but this time he made international news. Despite all the jokes and criticism, Italians know that they have one of the best pure strikers in Europe and that he is of considerable value to the national side if he is playing well.

Totti, however, continues to cause people to question his judgment. For example, what was he thinking when he recently passed up an opportunity to play for Real Madrid and chose to sign a deal with Roma that will have him playing there until 2010? Normally, if a player's home club is not doing well for several years, he tends to look to other teams that have a chance at winning championships.

Ever loyal to his Roma club, Totti must now focus on turning his club into challengers in the Serie A League and keeping his temper under control for the Azzuris in the 2006 World Cup in Germany. Either way he chooses to go, it is certain that he will be entertaining to watch the entire way.

Gianluigi Buffon
The Most Expensive Keeper

The goaltender stands stoically at one end of the field, watching the game unfold and only getting involved for a few brief seconds when he is required to make the most acrobatic saves, then return to a contemplative state while his teammates carry the ball back up the field. A goaltender can get all the glory with one simple save, or he can have the entire weight of losing the game placed on his shoulders. These kinds of pressures motivate a goaltender like Gianluigi Buffon to become one of the best ever to play between the pipes.

The Italian national chose his position by a twist of fate. Up to the age of 12, Buffon had always played as a midfielder and had never thought seriously about playing in goal. All that changed when he watched the Cameroon national soccer team make their historic run in the 1990 World Cup. No one expected the African team to make any inroads into the tournament, but their players won the hearts of fans around the world as they gave some of the stronger teams a run for their money in each game they played. In a World Cup that was noted for its overly defensive play, the Cameroonian team played an open attacking style of game that had the crowds cheering for the underdog. Included in their new-found fan base was a skinny 12-year-old boy from Carrara, Italy.

"I was a big fan of Cameroon. N'Kono (Cameroonian goalkeeper) was their symbolic, totemic player. I experienced this lighting strike, if you like," said Buffon in an interview with *Champions* magazine as he looked back at the beginnings of his passion for goaltending. "I decided to give it at least a year at being a goalkeeper. When I went in goal when playing with friends, I did quite well. After that I always stayed in goal."

Just a few years later, after making the switch to goalkeeper, Buffon was scouted by Parma for their junior league team. He made his debut on the Parma Serie A squad at the age of 17 in 1995 against AC Milan, and he was an instant success. After a decent year with Parma, Buffon made his first appearance playing for the Italian national team for the U-21 squad in the European Championships in 1996. When he returned from his stint with the national team to start the 1996–97 season, he had performed so well that the Parma management made him, at 19, the number one goaltender for the team. Most goalkeepers usually understudy a veteran for several years before they can cut their teeth as a team's first choice, but Buffon took to the number one position naturally.

As goaltender for Parma, he helped the team along with other young notables Hernan Crespo and Lilian Thurman to the UEFA Cup, Coppa Italia and the Supercoppa in 1999. His early successes with the national team and with his club set Buffon up for criticism from the media, who had come to expect miracles from the acrobatic goaltender.

"Because at 17 I started playing in Serie A, at 19, I played for the national side. It would have been fair to allow me to make mistakes. Instead there was, in my view, excessive criticism of me," said Buffon.

Looking past the criticism of his play, Buffon quickly became a fan favorite with his key saves and eccentric personality. On several occasions, he arrived on game day wearing a Superman t-shirt, to the raucous applause of the fans. They gave him the nickname "Superman" because of the way he flew through the air to make a save without fear of hurting himself on the landing. Buffon earned his superman reputation with skill that comes partly from his six-foot-three frame and amazing athletic ability but mostly from the way he is able to read and interpret how the game will develop and where the attackers are likely to place a pass or shot.

Veteran Italian goalkeeper trainer Ermes Fulgoni classified Buffon's style: "He understood new things, techniques we worked on in training, straight away. At Parma we worked on how to interpret the game and to decide when and where to intervene, how to beat an attacker to a ball. He is great at reading the game."

When the 2000 European Cup rolled around, it was a given that Buffon would be the starting goaltender. He started in seven of Italy's qualifying matches but was ruled out of playing in the tournament when he broke his thumb in one of the last qualifying games. It was a major blow to Buffon, who had worked hard to reach the number one goaltender position only to have it taken away because of a broken thumb. Luckily his thumb healed quickly, and he regained his title as number one goaltender for the Azzurri.

After a frustrating season with Parma in 2000–01, Buffon started entertaining offers from other clubs. He wanted to at least have a chance at winning the Champions League, and he knew that he would not get that with Parma. Manchester United and Barcelona were just two of the teams that made offers for the star goalkeeper, but the $33-million asking price scared off most potential candidates, most of whom had never paid that high a price for a goalkeeper. Eventually, the only team left at the negotiating table was the strong Italian Club Juventus. The team needed a replacement for the recently departed Edwin Van der Saar.

His first season with Juventus did not go as Buffon had planned. He made several errors in key games throughout the season, hurting the team's chances at winning the Italian league title. Despite his opening-season blunders, Buffon was back on track the next season earning those millions of dollars. His stellar performances during the season helped Juventus take the Italian Serie A league championship, a first for the now-veteran goalkeeper.

In the 2002–03 season, Buffon had a chance to make his soccer dreams come true when Juventus battled their way through the Champions League elimination rounds and were set to face Serie A rivals AC Milan in the final. The game was its usual defensive affair as Milan and Juventus traded a few rare chances on net and both keepers made key saves to keep the game tied at zero. The game was forced into the dreaded penalty shoot-out after extra time solved nothing. Shooting from just a few feet out in front of the net does not really favor the goalkeeper who can only make saves when he guesses the right direction of the shot. Buffon did not correctly guess often enough, for Milan was up 4–3 when David Trezeguet stepped up to the penalty area. Unfortunately for Juventus, Trezeguet missed his shot, sending AC Milan players streaming on to the field in celebration. Buffon lay slumped on the field, distraught at coming so close to winning one of the most cherished trophies in European soccer.

Buffon is still on the hunt for the bigger prizes in soccer. He came within one penalty goal of winning the Champions League, but he still hasn't come close to winning a major international tournament with the national team. Italy has consistently under-performed on the world stage, bowing out early in the 2002 World Cup against the Republic of Korea and not living up to expectations in Euro 2004. As a goalkeeper and as a private individual, Buffon takes each loss personally, but he relishes the challenge of the big tournaments.

"I need to have these big matches, the big stage," said Buffon. "The bigger the stimulus, the better. Yes, the nicer it is."

The next big challenge for Buffon will be to try to lead the national team far into the 2006 World Cup in Germany.

Arjen Robben
The Dutch Master

The 20-year-old Dutch national striker Arjen Robben is not generally thought to be one of the game's great players, but when Robben is in full flight on the field, he is a joy to watch and, for opponents, impossible to stop.

Despite nagging injuries that have plagued Robben throughout his career, he is a constant threat on the field. While he is often compared to other great Dutch players such as Johan Cruyff, Robben has added to his position his own style— a mixture of Dutch skill with a little Brazilian inventiveness. Robben can get past defenders with a quick crossover or a patented Cruyff turn (a move that looks like the striker is going to pass the ball but quickly hooks the ball backwards away from the defender hopefully toward open field) and find teammates with pinpoint accuracy. Not only does Robben excel at individual skills, he also is an excellent team player with great vision on the field.

Robben began his professional career in the Dutch League with FC Groningen but only received high praise when he moved to the stronger club, PSV Eindhoven, where he was a regular threat (scoring a career-high 12 goals in 33 games in the 2002–03 season). However, it wasn't until the next season that people really began to notice the young Dutchman.

The 2004 European Cup saw Robben catch the eye of the scouts from all the major teams in Europe. His skill and team play helped the Dutch side reach the semifinals before losing to host Portugal, but the striker's performance was enough to start a bidding war between two teams interested in acquiring his talents. Manchester United put in the first bid for Robben, but Chelsea ended up winning the battle for the young player. Manchester's first bid of $8.8 million was considered highly undervalued by the PSV management given his young age and obvious talent, and it was promptly rejected. Chelsea came to the table with a $22-million-offer, and Robben signed immediately.

"This is a great signing for Chelsea," said the club's Chief Executive Peter Kenyon who helped ink the deal. "Arjen is a top quality player who will become a major asset for our club in the years ahead. For his age, he shows great maturity and mental strength to go with his natural footballing skills. It's an excellent example of how Chelsea is appealing to the new wave of European talent and our commitment to bring the best young players to Stamford Bridge as well cultivate the best, young English talent."

The excellent movement, vision, dribbling skills, and pace that Robben's brought to Chelsea was an immediate asset to the team they were trying to build and would fit well into the plans of coach Jose Mourinho. Robben looked forward to the challenge of living in another country and playing another style of football.

"The pace of football is quicker in England than in Holland, and the physical challenges are a lot fiercer, but in general I play the same way I did at FC Groningen and PSV," said Robben in an interview with *Soccer Digest*. "Another difference is the pressure. Because of the mass attention, people have very high expectations. But I have no problems with that."

After he injured his ankle, his triumphant debut with Chelsea had to wait until a few months into the 2004–05 season. He would not make his debut until October, in a game against the Blackburn Rovers that Chelsea won 4–0. Robben's first goal with Chelsea finally came in a Champions League game against CSKA Moscow. He had broken the ice with his new club, but before he could get into any kind of playing rhythm, he injured himself again and was forced to sit on the sidelines while his Chelsea teammates dominated the English Premier league without him.

"It's hard being on the sidelines—you have no way of using up your energy and get frustrated because you want to prove yourself, especially when you're playing for a new club," said Robben.

Fortunately, Robben wasn't kept warming the bench for the entire season, and he returned in time to help his team with their last push for the English Premiership title as they edged out rivals Arsenal and Manchester United for English supremacy. The favorite in the Champions League finals, Chelsea was taken out of the tournament by league rival Liverpool on a controversial goal that still has people talking today.

Chelsea coach Jose Mourinho knew that the semifinal match against Liverpool was not going to be easy, but he knew that his players were ready, having played Liverpool several times that year in the Premier league. "We were well prepared for Liverpool," said Mourinho, looking back at the game.

They were not prepared for what happened at the four-minute mark of the game. Liverpool's Luis Garcia got a shot off from near the penalty area that rocketed off the crossbar behind keeper Petr Cech and then appeared to bounce behind the goal line and back out into the penalty, all in a fraction of a second. Both Chelsea and Liverpool supporters held their breath, unsure whether Garcia had actually scored. All the players turned their heads in unison towards the referee, who hesitated a moment as he replayed the shot in his head. When he made the signal that the goal counted, Liverpool went wild. Robben and the Chelsea players lowered their heads and walked off the field.

"You need a little luck to win things, and I'm sure many people would agree that's what we were lacking a bit when we lost to Liverpool in the semis," said Robben.

"Liverpool had a mixture of luck and merit and won with a goal that never was," said Mourinho.

On the international stage, Robben hopes to continue the rise of the Dutch squad and to improve on their semifinal showing at Euro 2004. Playing beside Ruud Nistelrooy and with a quality keeper in Edwin van der Sar, the Dutch have on paper a good team that can compete with the more established teams like Portugal, Spain and Germany. Once the qualifying rounds are finished, Robben is eager to show what his team can bring to the competition.

At 21, Robben has barely scratched the surface of what he will do on the international stage and in the English Premier league. And if the injury bug can stay away long enough, he will be converting new fans and making new enemies on the field with every touch of the ball.

Ruud Van Nistelrooy
Goal Scorer's Touch

The Manchester United star and Dutch national Ruud Van Nistelrooy did not start his life with a passion for soccer like most professionals. In his early years, he trained as a gymnast. Gymnastics is not the usual background for one of the best strikers in the English Premier league, but the training served him well on the field, giving him a unique athletic ability and a sense of balance unlike any other soccer player.

Born in 1976, in the Holland town of Oss, Van Nistelrooy found the game of soccer a little later than most, but once he put the ball at his feet, it was obvious that he had talent. That talent was finally noticed when Dutch club FC Den Bosch signed Van Nistelrooy to his first professional team in 1992. Van Nistelrooy spent the next four years with the lower league club, perfecting his skills before being called up to the first division team Heerenveen in 1997, where he scored 13 goals that season. Top Dutch league team PSV Eindhoven noticed the young 21-year-old striker's natural ability in the penalty area and his goal-scoring touch, and they signed him the next season to an $8.4-million contract.

With PSV Eindhoven, Van Nistelrooy became the standout player that he is today. He was able to perfect his skills not only as a striker but also as a leader on and off the field. The change made a marked difference in his goal output, scoring 31 goals in his first season with PSV. That same year, Van Nistelrooy made his first appearance with the Dutch national team and was named Holland's soccer player of the year.

Van Nistelrooy was riding high on his recent success with the national team and with PSV. Unfortunately, at the end of the 1999–2000 season in a friendly match with another Dutch club, Van Nistelrooy injured his knee. It was bad timing because Manchester United had scouted the Dutch national and offered him a contract with the team on condition that he pass a physical. But because of his knee, he was unable to meet the request, and his move to the English super club had to be postponed.

With his season in a shambles, Van Nistelrooy had to wait until April 2001 before signing with Manchester United for the sum of $27 million. Van Nistelrooy quickly found his place on the team as the go-to guy for the accurate crosses of David Beckham, whom he combined with on many occasions, scoring 23 goals in 32 games and adding another 10 goals in Champions League play. The 2002–03 season saw him put up the same results as the previous season and solidify his place on the team. Many critics questioned whether he would continue to be as effective when Beckham was traded to Real Madrid of the Spanish League, but Van Nistelrooy's successes continued even after Beckham's departure, silencing the critics that said he was a by-product of Beckham's skill.

Van Nistelrooy's prolific goal scoring comes from his unique ability to always be in the right place at the right time. He has scored countless goals on simple tap-ins and headers, but he is equally comfortable with one-on-one challenges and acrobatic shots from all angles. Every time he is on the field, he places himself in the best spot for his midfielder to hit him with a pass. He seems to have a sixth sense as to where the best place is on the field, and he is there before the ball. In his first three seasons with Manchester United, Van Nistelrooy scored his 100th goal by February of 2004.

His knee injury once again came back to haunt him, and he was forced to sit on the sidelines for most of the season, only playing in 27 games.

"It was a massive blow because I was desperate to get back playing after the disappointment of Euro 2004. But you have to take the good with the bad, and injuries invariably hit you at the wrong time and when you least expect them. But now I'm back, that disappointment has subsided," said Van Nistelrooy.

Despite these setbacks, the Dutch prolific scorer still managed to put away 16 goals that season.

Van Nistelrooy also found a new partner at the forward striker position in young phenom, Wayne Rooney. Those critics who said Van Nistelrooy's scoring prowess would fizzle after the departure of Beckham were proven completely wrong as the two have combined, when healthy, to be one of the best striker tandems in the Premier league.

The scary thing about watching Van Nistelrooy play is that he makes the most difficult moves look easy. His goals come often, but they are never the spectacular goals of a Zidane or a Ronaldinho. His game is natural and pure technique. His work in the penalty area is similar to that of Real Madrid striker Raul, who also has a natural ability to be in the right place at the right time and has a touch on the ball that is both delicate and accurate at the same time.

Van Nistelrooy's remarkable success has made the Manchester United striker one of the most sought-after players in the European Leagues and rumors of a trade constantly surround the Dutch national. He has been linked on several occasions with a trade to the star-filled Real Madrid, but his recent contract extension with Manchester until 2008 silenced most trade speculation.

"It just carries on, all these transfer rumors about me signing for Real. I still haven't found the source, but I think it all comes from Spain," said Van Nistelrooy, who is frustrated at the constant attention surrounding his team loyalty. "I really don't care what people claim and say about me going to Madrid. I just know it is not true. The manager knows it is not true, the players know it is not true, but the fans are getting more and more restless because of all these persistent transfer rumors."

With his place at Manchester assured until 2008, Van Nistelrooy would like nothing more than to add to the list of successes with a title win for the Dutch national team. The last time Holland won a major competition was the 1988 European Cup. The entire nation turned orange (the color of their flag) with pride for those few weeks as every soccer fan was glued to the televisions and radios. For Van Nistelrooy, it would be the perfect complement to a career filled with club successes.

"The Dutch team has a magic flavor to me. I don't play for the money. I am after winning a big trophy and big honors with Holland," said Van Nistelrooy. "All the players of the Dutch squad were young boys when Holland won the European Championship in 1988 in Germany. Now we all want to do the same thing. We have a chance to do it. Every player is aware of that."

With players like Arjen Robben, Roy Makaay and Van Nistelrooy, the Dutch are one step closer to victory at the 2006 World Cup in Germany and, with Van Nistelrooy's recent marriage, things are looking better and better for one of the best strikers in the world.

Christiano Ronaldo
Mercurial Touches

The Portuguese national and Manchester United superstar Christiano Ronaldo has the world at his golden feet, and he's just entered his 20s. Spend a few moments watching Ronaldo move the ball between his golden boots (literally painted gold), and you will see why this rising star has earned the respect of his teammates and opponents across the soccer world.

Perfecting his skills at an early age on the Portuguese Island of Madeira, Ronaldo quickly became a force. As word of the young phenom's skill spread to the mainland, scouts from across Europe started knocking on his door. At 15 years old, Ronaldo was too young and needed a few more pounds in order to be taken seriously on the field, but his sheer talent was clearly visible. At 17 he began his career with Sporting Lisbon (to rave reviews), but he still needed to work out the kinks in his game.

One coach said of Ronaldo in his early days: "Watching Ronaldo is like going to a football match and a circus in one."

The description is valid. While a player like David Beckham is known for his play-making ability and vision of the field, Ronaldo's talent is on the ball. Ronaldo considers soccer an art, and he constantly practices new tricks and moves to try out on the field. Add this large bag of tricks to the fastest and lightest feet in soccer, and you have one deadly force on the pitch. Ronaldo seems to glide across the field on the tips of his toes, working his way around players who are caught trying to figure out where the ball might end up as Ronaldo speeds by them with a lighting-fast three-stepover move.

After moving up to the Sporting Lisbon club, Ronaldo's talents were noticed by a wider audience. After several years of developing his skills with the Lisbon squad, Ronaldo played one fateful game against Manchester United that marked him for the next decade as a star player. Unaccustomed to the individual skills and flare of the Portuguese league, Manchester United players looked like they had rocks in their boots as Ronaldo staged a clinic on football artistry and control. Sir Alex Ferguson, coach for Manchester United, immediately liked what he saw in the skinny attacker and, a week after the game, Ronaldo was signed at a cost of $20 million as a possible replacement for the recently departed David Beckham.

"After we played Sporting, the lads in the dressing room talked about Ronaldo constantly," revealed Ferguson. "And on the plane back from the game, they urged me to sign him—that's how highly they rated him."

Not everyone was sold on the young Ronaldo and his mercurial feet. For some, individual skills were seen as all show with no substance; he was accused of showing off and playing to the fans. It took Ronaldo some time to get used to the English style of soccer, but within a few games the criticism quickly turned into quiet interest and finally into full-out admiration for the young Portuguese star and his artwork on the field.

Ronaldo has put on some weight since joining United and has adapted himself to their system of play, working alongside Wayne Rooney and Ruud Van Nistelrooy. Using his vast repertoire of tricks and dekes, he's able to make room on the field for a pass or shot on net. Ronaldo's six-foot one-inch frame helps him inside the penalty area. He has scored several beautiful headers, something he was not previously known for during the past two seasons. But for Ronaldo, it's all about progress.

"I don't like people copying my tricks. I would never, for example, copy Ronaldinho if I saw him doing something on the pitch," said Ronaldo in an interview with Champions magazine. "I see football as an art, and all players as artists. Different tricks come naturally to gifted players, and we must concentrate on developing our own natural talents rather than try and be someone else."

One thing is certain about the young Portuguese phenomenon, he will just keep getting better and better. For now he can just dream of what might happen. "My dream is to be European champion with club and country and win the World Cup with Portugal," said Ronaldo.

No one doubts that he can do it.

Luis Figo
The Elder Statesman

Now considered an old man by professional soccer standards, Luis Figo has been a dominant force on the field since his professional debut some 15 years ago. He has shown few signs of slowing down.

Sharpening his skills on the streets of the Lisbon neighborhood where he grew up, Figo's talent was recognized at an early age. He was signed up to the junior squad of the famous Sporting Lisbon franchise at the age of only 11. He joined the professional Sporting Lisbon club in 1989 and had an immediate impact on the team's success.

On the national team, Figo was an instant success, winning the Under–16 European Championships in 1989 and the U-20 World Championships in 1991. That same year he joined the senior Sporting Lisbon club and honed his talents until the larger clubs came knocking at his door. After winning the Portuguese Cup with Sporting Lisbon in 1995, Figo's contract was bought out by FC Barcelona.

In Barcelona, Figo went from a quality player to superstar status under the guidance of legendary coaches Johan Cruyff, Bobby Robson and Louis van Gaal. They trained the young Portuguese national to use not only the dribbling skills and tricks he already had, but to understand how play develops on the field and how to take advantage of the right moments when given the opportunity. Not a direct striker like a Ruud Van Nistelrooy or Adriano, Figo plays to the outside of the field where he is able to get a good view of the play and, given his dribbling skills, perhaps cut across the defenders in order to get a shot at the net. The hesitant style might make him look slow, but Figo is quick to run past many unsuspecting defenders.

Figo became one of the Barcelona favorites in his years with the club, so the announcement that he had been signed to Real Madrid came as a shock to the Barca faithful. He had led the team to several Spanish League titles and was the backbone of the regenerated Barcelona squad that had been languishing in the basement of the league before his arrival.

Real Madrid's new boss, Florentino Perez, had attained his presidency on the promise that he would bring stars like Figo to the team in order to get the team back to the top of the league. When Figo made the move, newspapers and television in Barcelona vilified the Portuguese striker, saying that he had betrayed the team that made him. Unfazed by the criticisms coming from the Barcelona fans, Figo began his first season with Real Madrid by justifying his $60-million-transfer by helping the club to the league title and the Champions League title in 2002. He also collected for himself the FIFA World Footballer of the Year award for his outstanding play on the field.

Former Real coach Jupp Heynckes described Figo's style and charisma with the fans, "Luis is technically perfect, quick off the mark and a great dribbler. He's a striker who pulls the crowds into the stadium."

Perez's idea of signing high profile superstar players seemed to be working as Figo proved that the "galacticos" (superstar) system showed significant signs of improving the team. Figo has been named Spain's favorite player several years in a row, but through all the publicity and attention he tries to retain some semblance of a normal life. Like David Beckham, Figo is often highly criticized when he doesn't meet the high expectations people have for him. Yet, Figo remains calm in the face of criticism. As one of the older guys on the field, he has seen all aspects of the game, good and bad.

"We are so used to Figo playing brilliantly that we think he's playing badly when he just plays normally," said Jorge Valdano, Real Madrid's technical director.

Off the field, Figo is married to Swedish model Helene Swedin, and they have one child. He is rarely in the local gossip papers because he likes to keep a low profile, preferring to stay home and read a book or chat with friends while hanging out on the beach. He seemed to have everything going for him in 2004, so it came as a shock to the soccer world when he announced his retirement from international competition.

"At the right time I will have to make my choice. I think the time has come to take a break. I don't know if it will be forever, because I will never refuse to serve my country and because no one can predict the future, but at this moment I feel the need to stop. If I am still active and fit, of course I would like to play in the (World Cup) finals in Germany in 2006, but before that we have the qualifiers," said Figo in a 2004 interview, revealing his uncertainty of his soccer future.

However, with the return of players like Zidane from international retirement, Figo changed his mind and decided to play for the Portuguese national team in Germany for the 2006 World Cup alongside newcomers like Cristiano Ronaldo and

Ricardo Quaresma. Hopefully, they will bring the World Cup home to Portugal for the first time.

"Figo is a great player who has a lot to give to the Portuguese team in every respect," Portuguese coach Luiz Felipe Scolari said. "He will be received with open arms."

Portuguese soccer fans were delighted to hear that their champion would be returning to lead the team in the 2006 World Cup one last time. They saw this as a chance to redeem themselves after their disappointing loss to Greece in the final at the European Cup in 2004. All eyes will be watching to see if he still has enough magic left to return to his country a champion and to bring his new team, Inter Milan, to the heights of the Italian Serie A League.

Raul
Captain Madrid

Raul, born Raul Gonzalez Blanco, has played his entire career with Real Madrid and has seen the team through its finest moments in recent years. Since his debut with the club in 1994, Raul has won several Spanish Liga titles, has been the recipient of countless awards and has raised the Champions League Cup above his head three times. No matter how impressive his resume might be, however, his real talent is on the field as captain of one of Spain's most popular teams.

Raised on Madrid football, Raul got his start with Athletico Madrid, but when the club was experiencing financial trouble, the young striker was quickly scooped up into the Real Madrid system. He eventually made his successful professional debut in the 1994–95 season. When Real's coach Jorge Valdano introduced Raul into the starting lineup at 17, the youngster did not disappoint; he scored six goals in his first 11 games. Considering that his six goals came at a time when Raul was at midfield for most games, it was quite the surprise to many doubters that the 17-year-old could score as he did. Eventually, his scoring ability forced the coach to move him from midfield to forward striker as the forward primary playmaker.

Despite his early success, Raul was not chosen for the national team for the 1996 Euro Cup because coach Javier Clemente thought he was too young and inexperienced. While it would be another two years before Raul graced the field for the Spanish national side, he continued to tear up the field with Real Madrid, quickly becoming the talk of Madrid. Photographers and journalists hoping to find dirt on the young star followed his every move. Fueled by a nation of young girls wanting to know everything about the newest bachelor on the scene, Raul was and still is one of the most famous people in Spain. Unfortunately, young girls across the country had their hearts broken when he met and married model Mamen Sanz. She is still in his life today, and fans might notice that every time he scores a goal he kisses his wedding ring as a salute to his wife.

Through all the flashbulbs and gossips columns, Raul has remained steady on the field. He won the Spanish Liga title in 1995 and 1997, the World Club Cup in 1998, and was one of the main reasons that Real Madrid won the Champions League title in 1998. Add the team titles to the individual titles he has won over his career, and the list of his accomplishments is impressive.

Raul's home on the field is in the penalty area. He has an incredible ability to foresee where his teammates will place a cross or where a rebound will fall (somehow always between his feet). Raul is a versatile striker but needs to be fed and directed with a good midfielder that can place passes near him in the penalty area. He almost always scores when he gets his foot on the ball, but he rarely produces goals by dribbling with a fancy trick past defenders. His skill and grace on the field have earned him some of the highest praises from the best players and coaches in the game.

"At the moment, he is one of the greats of our time. He crosses very good, and he is number one in mobility, his capacity to score, and what surprises me most is that he has stayed more than five years at an extraordinary level... Raul is a 'monster,' he has much talent, there is no doubt but it is very early still for comparing him to Di Stefano," said Pele, before Raul broke Di Stefano's record of 49 goals in Champions League play.

"Raul is a key player for us; he is a leader, a 'prodigy.' Although he is young, he is our chief on the ground, and one of those who contaminates the others," said Real Madrid teammate Roberto Carlos.

While his achievements for Real Madrid have made him one of the most feared strikers on the field in league play, he has yet to show his talents while playing for the Spanish national team. After his disappointing performance in his first World Cup appearance in 1998, Spain made further advances in Euro 2000 and the 2004 World Cup, but the Raul that is famous for his goal-scoring in league play has failed to translate that ability to the international stage. For the 2006 World Cup in Germany, Spain's chances are a little better with a set of new young players like Cesc Fabregas, Jose Antonio Reyes and Ivan de la Pena. The national side has not performed well in past tournaments, always seeming to buckle under pressure and failing to live up to the expectations of a nation so passionate about the sport.

Since winning the Spanish league title and the UEFA best striker award in 2003, Raul's quality of play has diminished along with Real Madrid's fortunes. Since club president Florentino Perez began signing some of the best soccer players that money could buy, the pressure has been on players like Raul to perform up to the extremely high standards of the fans and coaches. Nicknamed the "galacticos" because of their superstar status, the team, featuring Raul, David Beckham, Zinedine Zidane, Ronaldo, Roberto Carlos, Robinho, and a few others, has not lived up to their potential since they last won the Spanish league title. Perez's plan to buy the best players seems to have backfired, but they have started the 2005–06 season off well, and the possibilities for the team are tremendous.

"People say the galacticos era is over, but that is far from the truth," said Raul. "Next season we will prove that. I am sure Real Madrid will be the best team in the world again, and I will be back at my best."

The people of Madrid and Spain will be watching their favorite player to see if he lives up to those promises.

Xavi Hernandez Creus
Catalan Favorites

Xavier Hernandez Creus, or Xavi as he is more commonly known, is not a typical soccer player. He doesn't score many goals at his midfield position, his shot is not the strongest on the field and he can't dribble anything like teammate Ronaldinho. Xavi's importance to the team is based on his amazing vision of the field and his ability to make split-second, one-touch decisions. His ability might not seem like an attribute that would be essential to a top-level team, but his touches and passes are what lead to many Barcelona goals.

Xavi has been part of the FC Barcelona since he was first signed to the team when he was 11 years old as part of their junior training program. He finally got his debut with the first team in 1998 in a Spanish Super Cup game against Mallorca. In an unforgettable debut, he scored in his first professional game and secured himself a regular position on the first team. Xavi played an integral part that year in helping his squad to the league title in the 1998–99 season. He played in his first full season when regular midfielder Pep Guardiola left Barcelona to play in the Italian Serie A, opening up the 35-game season to Xavi. It was especially significant for Xavi to earn a place on the team since he was born in the Catalan region, and Barcelona had always been his favorite team.

As the fortunes of Barcelona went up and down under a succession of coaches, Xavi was placed in several positions on the field as they tried to make use of his defensive talents and keep him close to his goal. But Xavi, a natural playmaker, soon found his way back onto the attacking midfield, where he found instant success. He learned a lot in his early days from head coach Louis Van Gaal and Barca assistant coach Jose Mourinho.

"You would think he is an arrogant so-and-so, but actually he is a great guy. He helped me a lot," said Xavi about the much-maligned and controversial coach Mourinho. "He helped me to become a proper professional footballer. I used to talk a lot about soccer with Mourinho; he knows what he is talking about. Among the players we used to say, 'this guys knows.'"

Xavi has used instruction from Mourinho and Gaal to become the go-to playmaker on the Barcelona squad, more than replacing the hole left by Guardiola. Several teams have offered Xavi sizeable sums to move to their teams, but he has always refused the offers as long as he has a successful place with his team. He was born in the region, he grew up cheering for the fortunes and misfortunes of Barcelona and he has been part of FC Barcelona since he signed to their junior training club. Why would he leave when things are going so well?

"I like what I see of myself, I don't deny that. I do not know where my limit is, but if I do not improve, I hope to maintain this level for some time," says Xavi.

Ronaldinho
The Golden Touch

The smile is unmistakable; the skill is legendary. Ronaldinho is the kind of footballer every coach would love to have. Football seems to course through his veins. His talent is instinctual, at times premeditated genius, and his Brazil and Barcelona squads have been more than grateful to have him on their team.

Ronaldinho, full name Ronaldo De Assis Moreira, was born March 21, 1980, in the Brazilian town of Porto Alegre. He knew from an early age that soccer was going to be a large part of his life and, as far back as he can remember, he has had a love affair with his favorite sport.

"It's the one thing I wanted to do as a child," said Ronaldinho in an interview in Champions magazine. "My first presents were a ball and mini boots, so I was encouraged to play at a very early age. I used to sleep and wake up with the ball. I would play with my friends, and after they got tired, I kept playing with my dog because he would never stop."

Ronaldinho quickly developed the size and skill that enabled him to get to his current level. But the path wasn't always a perfectly smooth one. Until he grew to his 5-foot-11 frame, the awkward young Ronaldinho didn't possess the ball-handling skills and surefootedness that he has today. Often, at the local football field, he was not chosen to play with the bigger boys who could dribble circles around him. It took him a few years to grow into his skin, but when he scored 23 goals in one youth game, heads began to turn toward quick-footed Ronaldinho. He gave his first press conference right after the game. From then on, he has maintained a steady rise to the top.

Football is to Brazil what hockey is to Canada. Young boys are brought up with a passion for the sport. While Canadians practice their hockey in freezing weather, Brazilians play football with a passion and sense of style that is as uniquely Brazilian as Carnivale. The Brazilian football world came to know the inventive Ronaldinho for the first time after his appearance at the World Under–17 Championships in 1997 in Egypt, where he scored two goals and made an impression on everyone who saw him play. Clearly, he would one day be a force to reckoned with.

The first professional team to recognize his talents was the popular local club, Gremio. They worked with him from an early age to develop his skill, and once it was felt he could hold his own against the larger players, Ronaldinho's talents were let loose on the opposing teams. His success was immediate.

His presence on the ball is ghost-like. His feet seem to move in every direction at once, making it almost impossible to judge which way he will run. He is a challenge for any defender to take down or grab the ball, and he has a solid shot that can challenge the best goaltender. He also possesses the creativity that makes his style of football uniquely Brazilian and all his own at the same time.

Those days spent on the dirt fields in his town of Porte Alegre, playing in unorganized matches, required more individual creativity than team systems. The essence of the Brazilian game comes from unique dribbles and flicks rather than from physical challenges and long-distance passes that are more native to the English style of play. Football and the samba are often mentioned in the same breath when people speak about Brazilian football style, and in recent years none have mastered such skills better than Ronaldinho. Just the way he speaks about football tells us that he was born to play.

"One move? I like 'the elastic,' as they call it in Brazil, where in a split second you caress the ball with the outside of your foot and then the instep," said Ronaldinho in an interview with the *Mirror*. His choice of words evokes a clear sense of his passion for the game: "I didn't invent this move personally. The first time I saw it used was by the great Rivelino, and I have just modernized it. I really wanted to do it; I fell in love with it."

In his second season with Gremio, he scored six goals in 19 matches, and in his third season scored eight goals in just 11 games. It was soon clear to everyone who followed football in Brazil that they would lose their beloved "Gaucho" to one of the richer European teams. But it wasn't just about the money. Fans knew that Ronaldinho was too good for the Brazilian league and that his talents would only improve in the higher-profile European leagues. But a better Ronaldinho meant a better Brazilian national team, so not many people complained about his inevitable move.

After sitting out six months while Gremio and his new Parisian club Paris Saint-Germain battled over his transfer fee, in 2001 Europeans got their first real look at the smiling Brazilian. He didn't completely break out of his shell, however, until the 2002 World Cup in Japan and Korea.

His first appearance against Turkey was less than spectacular, but shaking off the nerves for his second match of the tournament against China, Ronaldinho displayed his magic all over the field. Roberto Carlos scored the first goal on a free kick that Ronaldinho won. The second goal was scored off a Brazilian rush into the Chinese defensive zone. Ronaldinho and Rivaldo expertly exchanged a series of volleys before Ronaldinho caught

Rivaldo with a pass that he punted into the net for the second goal of the game. That goal seemed to take the life from the Chinese national team. The third goal came off the foot of Ronaldinho after he was brought down inside the penalty area by the Chinese defense. Ronaldinho calmly put the ball into the net and strolled off the field for the half-time break. The Brazilian coach, knowing that the game was under their team's full control, wisely rested his star player for the rest of the game and for the subsequent match against the Costa Ricans.

The goal of the tournament for Ronaldinho came in an important quarterfinal match against the mighty English team with players like David Beckham, Michael Owen and Paul Scholes. Two different approaches to the game were on display for the world to see, and Ronaldinho made sure his mark on the game was felt immediately. England got the early jump in the game with a goal by Michael Owen, but Brazil came back shortly after with a spectacular goal from Ronaldinho.

With Brazil attacking in strength in the English half of the field, the defenders were forced to fall back and play the ball aggressively. This tactic played into the hands of Ronaldinho, who got a free kick within striking range of the English net. Pulling away from the ball, Ronaldinho paused in order to keep the goaltender guessing where he was going to place the ball. The crowd's noise at the stadium came in waves as Ronaldinho set himself for the free kick. What happened next was nothing less than spectacular. Ronaldinho ran up to the ball but instead of blasting it from where he was, hoping to beat the English goaltender to the open net, he kicked the ball in a wide arc that fooled everyone and tied the game at 1–1. The winning goal came on an assist off a beautiful run over the halfway marker when Ronaldinho burst by his attackers and got off a precise pass to an open Rivaldo for the match point. But the game was tainted for Ronaldinho when he was sent off for a vicious-looking tackle on David Beckham (it looked a lot worse than the replay showed). Having to sit out the semifinal match against Turkey, Ronaldinho returned to face the Germans in the World Cup final where he played well and, at age 22, became a World Cup champion.

The love affair with Paris St-Germain did not last forever. The young Brazilian seemed more interested in the nightlife of Paris than the action on the football field. When rumors began to emerge from Paris that the Brazilian national wanted a new team, Barcelona jumped at the chance to snap up Ronaldinho. Barcelona originally wanted Beckham but settled on Ronaldinho as the second prize at $36 million a season. It turned out to be the best decision for Barcelona because they climbed back to the championship of the Spanish league title.

With the 2004 FIFA World Footballer of the Year award under his belt, Ronaldinho still has his sights set high as he starts a new season with Barcelona and takes his beloved Brazilian national team to Germany to defend its title as the best football nation in the world. Many people will be cheering on the buck-toothed Ronaldinho for a long time to come, and he is certain to have a few tricks left up his sleeve.

"I believe that a football player continues to learn right up until he retires. I am still young, and I can still improve," said Ronaldinho. "They do say that 28 is the age when you are your best, and I am very pleased that I still have plenty of years ahead of me and a lot more to learn."

Kaka
Brazil's New Weapon

Adopting the one-name moniker has become a distinctly Brazilian way of identification on the playing field, and Ricardo Izecson Santos Leite, better known as "Kaka" (accent on the last syllable), has one of the most unusual names in national team history. Fittingly, he received this name from his little brother who couldn't pronounce Ricardo, so his brother called him Kaka, and the name stuck.

Apart from the colorful name, Kaka is one of the best talents to come out of Brazil since the arrival of Ronaldinho. He has a unique touch on the ball and is comfortable attacking from any part of the field. His powerful kick is something to behold when he unleashes a shot from just outside the goal crease, often leaving the keeper lying prostrate on the ground wondering how the shot got past him from that distance.

Through fame, money, and harsh media scrutiny, Kaka keeps himself grounded and level-headed through his ultra-Catholic faith. The baby-faced Brazilian prays everyday, wears a t-shirt beneath his jersey that reads "I belong to Jesus," has his soccer cleats engraved with the words "I am of Jesus" and even signs autographs with "God bless you." He never makes it into the daily newspapers with reports of girlfriends, clubs he's visited or the generally wealthy lifestyle that most soccer players lead.

His beginnings are not typically Brazilian either. Most stories of Brazilian players in their youth usually involve playing on cement fields late into the night, practicing the sport they love in hopes of finding a way out of the local slums. But Kaka, son of a civil engineer, had a typical middle-class upbringing that could have allowed him to excel in a multitude of careers. But "futebol" (Brazilian for soccer) was his passion and since his early teens, he has been a force on the field. His dreams almost went unfulfilled when, just one year before his professional debut with Sao Paulo, he broke a vertebra in his neck when he hit his head on the bottom of a swimming pool. Luckily, he was able to recover in a few months and continued to impress the scouts that came to see him.

In his first professional game with Sao Paulo, Kaka was sent on the field with a few minutes remaining in the game. His team was down 1–0 against rivals Rio de Janeiro. Kaka scored two goals in two minutes and was an instant favorite in the Brazilian media. He was labeled the next big thing in national soccer.

On the field, many expect to see the flashy individual style for which Brazilians have become famous around the world, but Kaka once again defies convention. Having always played behind the strikers, Kaka's style can adapt to the coach's needs, a talent that makes him a valuable asset on the Brazilian national team and with his club team AC Milan, both of which are filled with an excess of goal-scoring strikers.

"I'm not really too worried about how far forward or back I'm played," said Kaka. "If I start on the right, as is often the case at Milan, I can find more space."

This easy-going manner was not the Brazilian style that many were expecting to see from Kaka, but it is this versatility that makes him such a threat on the field. His arrival in Italy was met with some reservations by a skeptical media who stereotyped the youthful Brazilian as being all tricks and dribbling while having little in the way of substance. Within a short time, Kaka proved to the doubters that he could play a well-rounded game and still utilize the patented Brazilian trickery. The ability to play a quality game in most positions on the field has drawn comparisons to Brazilian legend Rai, who happens to be Kaka's role model and favorite player. Rai was the all-round player, able striker and a strong midfielder who could set up teammates in the penalty area with pinpoint passes.

With AC Milan, Kaka has found his niche on the team as an attacking midfielder behind strikers like Andriy Shevchenko and Christian Vieri, but Kaka, as he proved recently in a Champions League game against Turkish Fenerbahce, can also step up and become a striker as good as any on his team.

After Fenerbahce tied the game at the 63-minute mark on a penalty shot, Kaka stepped up with his second goal of the game. With the game coming to a close, Kaka slalomed his way past three defenders on the edge of the field, then broke just inside the penalty area and blasted a shot under the sprawled out keeper to put Milan ahead with the game-winning goal.

"They're comparing my goal to one of Maradona's? I didn't see him play very much, but I'm very happy to be compared with him," said Kaka after the match. "He was a great player who wrote his name into the history of football."

In just his third season with the Italian power-house club, Kaka is converting new fans each time he steps out onto the field. The skeptical Italian media, even after all this success, still deemed Kaka a one-hit wonder who couldn't perform up to AC Milan's standards. But the papers changed their tune quickly, dubbing him the "Prince of Milan" after Kaka won the Italian Serie A player of the year award for the 2003–04 season.

"Kaka is a true talent who is beginning to show his real class. Unlike other attacking midfielders he is able to score decisive goals," said legendary Brazilian player Leonardo. "One look at him, and you can see he's pure talent. The only risk was that he'd burn out, but instead, Kaka has shown he is mature even for our Serie A."

Internationally, things just keep getting brighter for the Brazilian national. Having already won a World Cup in 2002, Kaka is preparing himself for a new challenge in Germany for the 2006 version. With a lineup that has Kaka placed as the set-up man for players like Robinho, Ronaldinho, Ronaldo and Adriano, it is difficult to foresee any problems Brazil will have in defeating challengers. But, as Kaka knows from his losing experience in the Champions League final against Liverpool, you can never let your guard down no matter what team you're playing.

At 23, Kaka dominates the field whenever he plays. When he is either out with an injury or two players make it their business to shut him down, Kaka's entire team shuts down. Whether protecting midfield, leading a rush, or down low near the penalty area, Kaka is a threat on the field. All this talent, strength and sheer class, and AC Milan only paid $8.2 million for him. What a deal!

Adriano
The Definition of the Power Striker

When considering Adriano in the long line of stars to emerge from the Brazilian school of soccer, the large powerful striker breaks the mold with his amazing abilities on the field. People usually think of players like Ronaldinho and Robinho as the typical Brazilian soccer player. They follow the example of legendary players like Pele and Garrincha, whose styles on the field dominated soccer then and now. With Adriano, the creative style of players such as Ronaldinho is there, but he also brings another dimension to the game that makes the Brazilian national team an even more potent force.

Born Adriano Leite Ribeiro, in the soccer-mad city of Rio de Janeiro in the favelas (shantytowns) of the Vila Humeilde district, he was naturally drawn to soccer from an early age. Every free moment he had was spent thinking about or playing soccer.

"Football is my life. It has always been. But my parents didn't want me to play football. I had to go to school, to study, but in fact I studied so very little," said Adriano.

He spent most of his spare time on the local beaches playing pickup games with other local kids on the same field where Club Flamengo often practiced. Once into his mid-teens Adriano's skills had grown beyond the practice fields, and word spread quickly of his exploits on the field. Not only was the local press writing of his prodigious talents, he became just as well known for his physical presence on the field.

At 6 foot 3 inches, Adriano cuts an imposing figure on the field. Unlike many soccer players who are normally of a slimmer build, he is considerably larger than most strikers. Because of his size, in his early days, some thought that Adriano would not have the speed and skill of other smaller players, but he quickly proved that he could out-dribble and out-score the best of them.

Adriano made his national debut with the under–17 Brazilian national team in the 1999 World Cup in New Zealand, where he impressed enough people to be called up to play for Flamengo, the team he had always dreamed of playing for as a kid. In his first professional game, Adriano scored against Rivals Sao Paulo in a 5–2 victory.

Adriano used his time with Flamengo to turn his slightly chunky frame into a solid mass of muscle and perfect his light touch on the ball to the point that the more lucrative clubs from Europe began to take notice.

Many teams were interested in Adriano at the time, but Inter Milan of the Italian Serie A league was the club that won his contract for $17 million in 2001. In his first appearance with the team, in a game against Real Madrid playing for the Santiago Bernabeu Trophy, he nearly scored in the first half of the game on a beautiful header inside the box that just missed the inside post. He finally put one in the net (after several close chances) on a powerful free kick that blew by Madrid's keeper.

While the media was already placing him on a pedestal, Inter coaches were a little more skeptical, having seen many Brazilian players join teams with a lot of fanfare but quickly fizzle when the pressure of playing in Italy became too much. Adriano did anything but fizzle into obscurity; he continued to dominate whatever field he found himself on. Even with the fans' support and obvious skill on the ball, Inter coach Hector Cuper still remained hesitant about the striker's talents and only started Adriano in nine games in his first season.

In 2002 and 2003, he was loaned out to Fiorentina and Parma from Inter. After another season of waiting on the bench in Fiorentina, Adriano was sent off to Parma where he teamed up with Romanian Adrian Mutu. The tandem combined to become the highest scoring duo that year, scoring 15 goals, each off passes from one another. After coach Cuper was relieved of duty, Adriano was quickly brought back into the Inter fold halfway through the 2003–04 season, and he promptly scored 12 goals in 18 games.

Adriano was unlike the other Brazilian players in the Italian leagues at the time. He surprised many defenders and coaches alike with his quickness and agility on the ball. His strength has also gave him one of the most powerful shots in soccer. He has become a master of the free kick, not through technique but through sheer accuracy and power. Adriano truly excels around the penalty area where his size gives him a distinct advantage over many defenders. He is able to rise above the scramble of bodies on a cross and deliver accurate headers that leave the keepers on their toes any time he wanders into their vicinity.

At the Copa America (South American version of the Euro Cup), Adriano dominated the Brazilian score sheet, leading his team to the championship. He was named player of the tournament for his outstanding efforts and continued his record of impressive tournament showings at the 2005 Confederations Cup in Germany, leading Brazil to the final against long time rivals Argentina.

Brazil went into the game as the heavy favorite, and within the first few minutes of the match, it was apparent that the Argentine team was having trouble defending against the offensive skills of the Brazilian forwards. At just the 11th minute, Adriano took control of the ball and set the pace for the rest of the game. Coming down the right side of the field, Adriano didn't have many options before him. He was still held outside of the penalty area, and his teammates hadn't yet opened themselves up for a pass. Knowing that he had to make the play, Adriano faked one way then moved the ball onto his left foot. He blasted a shot from just outside the penalty area that found its way to the back of the net, right past the surprised Argentinean keeper who hadn't expected a shot on a dead-end play. Adriano later scored again on a header as Brazil defeated Argentina 4–1 to win the Confederations Cup. Adriano took home the player of the tournament award.

With such success, Adriano has become the topic of many trade rumors that would have him moving to teams with larger wallets like Chelsea, Real Madrid or Barcelona. But Adriano has always said that he would finish his career with one club. Rumors still abound, but Adriano has effectively put them to rest by signing a multi-year contract with Inter Milan until 2008.

"I would like to be to Inter what my idol Zico was for Udinese," Adriano said, referring to the famed Brazilian player who spent his entire career with Italian team Udinese.

Few people doubt that Adriano will succeed in the future. It's tough to predict just how high this versatile striker can climb with so much talent at his disposal.

Robinho
New Kid on the Block

The similarities are obvious and the accolades numerous, but they mean nothing if they don't come from the mouth of the man himself. So, when living Brazilian soccer-god Pele walked up to Robinho and told him that Robinho reminded him of himself when he was younger, Robinho's dreams had come true. The comparison is easily made. Both garnered the attention of the media when they were young. Both were skinny, black and raised in poor neighborhoods. While it might still be a few years before Robinho can claim to be on par with Pele's skills, both players have the creative control of the ball that deceives defenders and entertains supporters.

Robson de Souza, aka Robinho ("Little Rob"), was born in the town of Sao Vincente in Brazil and took to soccer like a Canadian boy to hockey. As soon as he could walk, he could be found with a ball between his feet. When there wasn't a ball to be had, he often rolled up socks and kicked them around for hours in the dirt of the soccer field, in his bare feet because he couldn't afford proper shoes. Life was tough from an early age for the young Brazilian, but he knew that if he practiced enough, he might one day play for the same team as his hero, Pele. By the age of nine, the skinny little kid from Sao Vincente was tearing up the local leagues for a team called Portuarios. (He scored 73 goals in five-a-side soccer in one season.)

His seemingly unending supply of tricks caught the attention of the famed Sao Paulo soccer club, Santos. The club signed him to the junior squad to see if his talent would hold up to some tougher competition. He not only held up against the players, but he made many of them look foolish as they stood dumbfounded while this skinny kid ran circles around them using all kinds of tricks and dribbling techniques. The management and the coaches for Santos knew immediately that this kid could not have been taught these skills; they were something he was born with—a gift from God. He was small, but the kid could play with the biggest of players.

His skills on the field proved to be so prolific that Santos called him up to the pro level when he was just 18. Robinho was an instant fan favorite of the Santos faithful. In his first year with the club, he helped his team get to the Brazilian national championship.

The final game had many standout players, but it was Robinho who put on the show for the crowd with dribbling skills that were remarkable for such a young talent. He performed a trick called the pedalada, a move that looks like his feet are pedaling above the ground. In this move, his feet never contact the ball until the defender becomes so confused about where Robinho's feet will go next that the defender barely has time to react before Robinho is already past him. Fans howled with delight every time he got his feet on the ball, and Robinho did not disappoint.

In the 2004 season, Robinho had his breakout year with Santos. He scored 21 goals in 36 matches in league play and was instantly thrown into the spotlight. Just before the end of the season, as Santos was set to clinch the league championship, Robinho received a phone call from the Brazilian police that would put a hold on his season and make him rethink whether his newfound fame was worth the trouble.

The police told him that his mother had been kidnapped from her home and taken for ransom. The criminals were threatening to kill his mother if Robinho didn't pay up. Robinho immediately left Santos and put the several European teams who had been interested in signing him on hold so that he could cooperate with the police and resolve the kidnapping. As a week passed with no news about the fate of Robinho's mother, the media began to speculate that she had been killed because of failed negotiations. Such rumors added more stress to an already tense situation for the young soccer star. All the speculation by the media proved wrong when police successfully negotiated the safe return of Robinho's mother. Details of the negotiations have never been released. Relieved that his mother was safe and under protection, he returned to Santos and helped them finish off the season and claim the league championship.

The kidnapping of sports stars' family members has become a common occurrence in some South American countries where gangs hope that celebrity status will bring a high ransom. Argentine tennis star David Nalbandian has received threats against his family, and Argentine soccer player Matias Almeyda moved back to Europe after he began receiving threats against his family. Some sports stars go so far as to hire personal bodyguards for their family members in order to secure their safety.

With his life back on track, Robinho could focus on the multitude of offers coming in from the European clubs anxious to sign him. Robinho was eager to sign on in Europe after the kidnapping ordeal and get his family to safety.

"At the moment I'm not in the right frame of mind to play in Brazil," said Robinho after the kidnapping. "It's difficult to say that I don't want to play for Santos any more, but that's how life goes."

All the major clubs started knocking on his door—PSV Eindhoven, Arsenal, Chelsea, Benfica.

"He is a player very much in demand, and his price has gone up in recent weeks," said Juan Figer, the Brazilian's agent.

But it was Real Madrid who made the most tempting offer of $36 million, and the opportunity to play with Brazilian teammates Ronaldo and Roberto Carlos sealed the deal for the young striker. At the Real Madrid press conference announcing the arrival of Robinho to the "galacticos" squad, the young striker was given the old number of the recently departed Luis Figo. His is a large reputation to live up to but one that the young star should have no trouble filling.

At the age of 21, Robinho has many years of soccer ahead of him and, with a team like Real Madrid on his side, he will only improve. His arrival in Europe has also established a permanent position for him on the Brazilian national team for the World Cup in 2006, making the Brazilians one of the toughest international teams in recent history. With players like Adriano, Ronaldo, Roberto Carlos, and now Robinho, they have a depth at all levels. And with the youthful creative talent of Robinho to take them to that next level, the team can possibly make history yet again with another World Cup victory.

Juan Roman Riquelme
At the Top

Born in the city of San Fernando in the Buenos Aires province of Argentina, Juan Roman Riquelme didn't have the opportunities that other kids had growing up in the richer areas, but he never cared about the luxuries of life as long as he had his family, friends and, of course, soccer.

Riquelme practiced everyday down at the local soccer field, working out his moves on imaginary players. Soon he was good enough to make the move to the organized local teams, where he dominated most players on the field. As word of his exploits on the field spread, scouts were soon knocking on his door, eager to sign the young Riquelme to their junior teams. River Plate and the Boca Juniors were the two teams he wanted to join, but Riquelme had always supported the Boca, so he enthusiastically signed up with them.

A year after signing with the youth squad, Riquelme played his first professional game for

Boca in 1996. It took just two weeks before the midfielder scored his first goal. He continued his career with the Boca Juniors for seven years before the European leagues got wind of his remarkable playmaking talents. Riquelme made a name for himself in the 2001 European/South American Cup when the Boca Juniors made it to the finals against European powerhouse Real Madrid. Some were expecting the Boca Juniors to put up a good fight in the final, but most predicted that Madrid would win the Cup. With Riquelme taking the lead, the Boca Juniors beat Real Madrid: shocking a soccer world that was certain the highly paid stars of Spanish soccer would beat the smaller-market team from Argentina. Riquelme instantly became a hot commodity for the larger European teams, and Barcelona was at the forefront of Riquelme's considerations. When he agreed to the $26-million transfer fee, he packed his bags for Spain and a new chapter in his career.

Things, however, did not continue on a high note for the Argentine national. Under the command of Barcelona coach Louis Van Gaal, Riquelme was placed out of his normal position as attacking midfielder and put in the defensive midfield, effectively taking his talent out of the game. Playing in 30 games in the 2002–03 season, Riquelme only scored three goals, far less than he had ever scored since starting his professional career. Unable to see the error of his ways, coach

Van Gaal never used Riquelme, and he was loaned out to league rivals Villareal.

With Villareal, Riquelme has found his place and is getting better with each game he plays. With Barcelona, he was forced to sit on the bench behind a lineup of quality players and did not have the opportunity to develop into the franchise player he has become with Villareal. He has helped the team come from the bottom of the Spanish league and qualify for the Champions Leagues 2005–06 season.

"With Villareal I have gained confidence and have been playing regularly. That's the essential difference. With Barcelona, I was never able to play continuously and no-one can improve like that," said Riquelme in a *FIFA* magazine interview.

Riquelme is a natural leader. His skills on the field give his team the ability to take forward chances and to commit an extra attacker on a rush, knowing that Riquelme will manage to avoid the defenders and hit them with a precision pass. With Riquelme on the team, Villareal plays a challenging game that can match the best teams in Europe. Remove the Argentine midfielder from the equation, and the team seems lost. His playmaking and defending abilities are so essential to the success of the team that they rarely win without him because they have to reorganize their system.

"If the team doesn't play well, it's because I didn't play well," said Riquelme.

He is so essential to the success of the team that Villareal bought out the remainder of Riquelme's contract from Barcelona and signed him to a four-year contract. Pairing Riquelme with Uruguayan striker Diego Forlan, Villareal has become a serious contender in every game they play.

The next challenge for Riquelme is making sure that the Argentine national team does well in the 2006 World Cup in Germany. After an excellent showing in the 2005 Confederations Cup—finishing in second place to winners and archrivals Brazil—Riquelme remains positive about Argentina's chances in Germany.

"Argentina are always under pressure to play well and win," said Riquelme. "We'll do our level best—all of us would like to see a top team. We want to win and play attractive football."

Whether he achieves his goals or not, one thing is certain: it will be entertaining to watch him at every stage.

Hernan Crespo
The Journeyman

Argentina, like Brazil, is mad about soccer. While Brazilian soccer has won the world over with its flamboyant style and colorful players, Argentina has remained right at its heels, producing some of the best players in the world. From this production comes one of the best rivalries in international sports. Hernan Crespo would watch his favorite players like Maradona battle on the field in World Cup games against Brazil and dream that one day he might wear the blue-and-white uniform and bring the championship to Argentina. He got one step closer to his dream when he made his first professional appearance.

Scouted and signed while he was still in his teens, Crespo has always been a danger on the field ever since he made his debut with Argentine club River Plate, scoring 13 goals in 25 games. His natural ability on the ball, his trickery and his amazing aerial skills make him one of the best strikers in the world today. With all that skill, one would think that teams would be lining up to have him on their team and keep him happy, but Hernan Crespo, once the most expensive man in soccer, has become the traveling journeyman of the soccer world, impressing wherever he goes but never staying too long in one place.

Crespo's debut with Argentine club River Plate was an excellent proving ground for the young striker. In his first year with the team, he helped them win the Apetura League Championship in 1993 and in 1994. His best year with the team came in 1996 when he helped River win the Copa Libertadores, the South American club championship, scoring twice to lead his team to victory. It wasn't long before the European clubs got wind of the Argentine national's significant talents as a striker and had him packing his bags for the first time when he was signed with Italian Serie A club Parma in 1996.

Crespo excelled at Parma, having some of the best years of his career with the Italian club. It's not easy for a young player to find himself suddenly playing soccer in another country, with another language and another culture, with no family to fall back on for support. His transition was made easier by learning the language and getting help from the other players, who took him under their wings and showed him what Italian life was all about. In his first season with the club under coach Carlo Ancelotti (now with Milan), Crespo helped the team to second place in the Serie A division, scoring 12 goals in 27 games. With each passing year, the young striker got better under the watchful eye of Ancelotti. Crespo scored another 12 goals the next season but improved to 16 and then 21 goals by 1999. The young Argentine striker's stock was rising in the soccer world, and he loved every minute of it.

"I am lucky to live this life, but I don't think I'm better than anyone else, especially not my friends," said 22-year-old Crespo after arriving in Parma.

His best year with Parma came in 1999 when he helped the club win the Italian Cup and the UEFA Cup. In the UEFA Cup final against French power-house Olympique de Marseilles, Crespo scored the opening goal in a 3–0 victory that surprised the French fans at the Moscow stadium. The Italian love affair with Crespo would continue when he was traded to Lazio in 2000, where he had his most productive goal-scoring season of his career in the notoriously defense-minded Italian league.

It is often said that if a player in the Italian leagues manages to score over 15 goals, he is a striker of true skill and quality because of the league's reputation for being overly defensive and low scoring. Crespo had just come off a great season with his former club with 21 goals and was expected to produce similar results for Lazio since they paid a record (at the time) $60 million for the striker's services. Lazio management got their money's worth that season for he led the league throughout the season in scoring with a career high of 26 goals. Unfortunately, Lazio never figured in any of the Serie A titles and were taken out early in the Champions League competition.

After two successful years with Lazio, Crespo had a brief appearance with Inter Milan. He was to serve as a replacement for the recently departed Ronaldo. However, Crespo only played 18 games, scored 7 goals and never really lived up to the expectations of the Inter coaches. The high salary was too much for the cash-strapped Inter team, so they shopped him around and found the rich Russian owner of Chelsea. He was interested in acquiring Crespo for the new team of superstars he was trying to build. With some reservations, Crespo signed and made the move to London.

Crespo's first season with Chelsea did not go as well as his time with the Italian clubs. In Italy, he felt at home in every city he played, able to get by with his poorly spoken Italian, but in England he couldn't speak the language and felt left out by the Chelsea management. In his first year with Parma, a young Crespo was welcomed to the team with open arms and given all the help he needed to acclimatize to his new environment. However, in Chelsea, as a veteran, he was left to his own devices. He felt isolated and, as a result, his play on the field suffered. He played only 19 games and scored 10 goals, results he was not used to getting.

"Depressed is a big word but when I finished the season, I thought seriously about not playing again," said Crespo in a BBC interview. "There was nobody to help me. I had personal problems. I was looking for an apartment. My English is not good. And when you change your country, don't speak the language and you feel alone, it's the worst thing."

With his family in Italy, it was difficult for the Argentine to settle in, so he was loaned out to AC Milan for the 2004–05 season, reuniting Crespo with his former Parma coach Carlo Ancelotti. Although his goal output was the same as with Chelsea, Crespo's season was far more successful, helping the team to the top of the Serie A division and scoring six goals in the Champions League finals. Milan lost the final game of the Champions League in a heartbreaker to Liverpool, but Crespo had regained some confidence in his game.

With the start of the new 2005–06 season, Crespo has returned to Chelsea under the guidance of Jose Mourinho and, this time, feels his place with Chelsea is more certain.

"I'm very happy that Hernan is coming back, and in sporting terms he is very happy to come back," said Chelsea coach Jose Mourinho.

Crespo echoed Mourinho's sentiments saying, "Chelsea now is a completely different club to the one of a year ago. They have gone forward in every respect and for me that is positive." The new season has started well for the Argentine national. He has scored several goals and is gaining the confidence of the Chelsea coach Jose Mourinho. His future in the English Premier League looks stable for the first time.

Crespo's national career has been just as successful as his club, for Argentina continues to be one of the dominant forces on the international scene. Crespo made his boyhood dreams come true when he began playing for his home country in 1995. He won a medal in his first major competition with the team in 1996, when Argentina won the silver medal in the Summer Olympics in Atlanta. Crespo finished the tournament as the top goal scorer with six goals. Since his debut, he has played in most major tournaments for his country and has scored 21 goals in his 42 appearances. Argentina hopes to bring back some of their successes from the past when the 2006 World Cup in Germany gets under way.

The dream final for many around the world would see Argentina against Brazil because of the rivalry that the two teams have built up over the years. The two titans of international soccer have a rocky history together on the field because both teams have faced each other numerous times in important games. There is no love lost between the two teams and their fans whenever the teams meet in competition. For the time being, Chelsea, Argentina and the world waits to see what Crespo will accomplish next.

Chapter Nine

AFRICA

Jay-Jay Okocha
Magic Man

Nigerian born, Jay-Jay Okocha has been delighting soccer fans since he burst onto the soccer scene with German League team Eintract Frankfurt. Then only 19 years old, Jay-Jay's excellent dribbling skills, outrageous tricks, and flamboyant goal celebrations made him a fan favorite. Some thought he wouldn't last long in the professional leagues with his flamboyant style, but he continues to leave audiences and defenders astounded at the level of his on-field trickery.

In his native country of Nigeria, not many opportunities exist for a skilled soccer player to make a living, unlike the players in the rich European leagues. In most African countries, a skilled player can only hope to break into the European markets where the base salary is far better than what he can earn at home. It was a risk to pick up and leave everything behind, but Okocha knew that he had the talent to make it in Europe. He entered Germany on a visitor's visa and took his chances at a tryout for the fourth division Borussia Neunkirchen Club and was immediately signed to the team. Just one year later, he was moved up to the first division and began making his name for himself across Europe. Okocha had come a long way from Nigeria, and he was going to go further.

Just two years after signing with the German Division, Turkish club Fenerbahce bought out his services. The team felt his impact immediately when they won the Turkish championship that same year. In his first season with Fenerbahce, Okocha had a career high record for goals with 16 goals in 33 games. After his next season, when he scored 14 goals, his value began to soar as teams across all leagues wanted to add the creative dribbling skills of the Nigerian midfielder to their arsenal. Okocha was traded to French club Paris St-Germain for $16.3 million in 1998. In just his second year with the club, he helped them to the League Cup finals in 2000, but his role on the team began to wane after some injuries and some fall-outs with people on the team. By the end of the 2002 season, Okocha had only played in 20 games and scored just four goals. Paris St-Germain wanted to shore up their midfield with a more consistent player, and Okocha was traded off to the English Premier Leagues Bolton Wanderers.

With Bolton, he has become a more all-round player, covering the midfield well and passing the ball into the penalty area for the strikers, as opposed to just a few years ago when he would have tried some flamboyant move to score on his own. The showman in Okocha is still alive, but he has now matured, and his naming as the Bolton captain has made him a more complete player.

In the English Premier league, Okocha no longer scored the number of goals he did with Fenerbahce, but his role on the team was still as important. When he is playing well, his flamboyant style can still spark his teammates into action, and his control of the ball around defenders enables him to get in the open to cross the ball to the strikers. When he is not playing well, he has often been criticized for not having the discipline and team-oriented style that would allow him to improve his game and compete at a higher level.

With Nigeria, or the Super Eagles as they are more commonly known, Okocha helped the team in the 1996 Olympic upset win over powerhouse Argentina. The win proved that African nations could produce a winning international team with exciting, attacking soccer. Okocha continued his successes with the Super Eagles, winning the African Nations Cup in 2000.

Okocha is one of the most successful African players of all time, having won Olympic gold, several league titles and the support of fans from his current club and from his home nation of Nigeria.

Didier Drogba
The Big Man Up Front

Born in the Ivory Coast city of Abidjan, Drogba moved to France at the age of five to live with his uncle, who was a professional soccer player in Brittany. After three years, Drogba moved back to Abidjan to live with his parents, but he returned to France when his parents fell on hard times so that he could have a better chance in the French education system. His parents joined him in France in 1991. Didier was failing at school, and his parents removed him from soccer as a punishment. Luckily, he got back on the field a year later and was tearing up the field in the suburbs of Paris, where his parents finally settled.

Drogba got his first taste of organized soccer when he was signed on to the local club, Levallois, where he trained under Srebencko Repcic, a former Yugoslavian international, who turned him into a pure, attacking striker. In two seasons, young Drogba scored 30 goals and was clearly on his way to higher levels in soccer once his age caught up with his skill level.

Drogba's skill on the field soon attracted the attention of the major French first division clubs like Paris St-Germain, Le Mans, and Guingamp, but Le Mans won the 19-year-old's contract.

Because of his size and incredible strength, the coach at Le Mans put him in the defender position when he first started out, but it soon became clear that his speed and skill on the ball could be used more effectively up front as in a striker's position. But it wasn't until his eventual move to Guingamp that he moved to the striker position full time.

His first year with the team was rather disappointing because Drogba only started in 11 games, scoring just three goals. The coach at Guingamp was not confident in the young striker and did not put him up front full time. Despite warming the bench for the 2001–02 season, Drogba stayed with the club, waiting for his chance to prove himself worthy of the first team. He did not disappoint in the next season, scoring 17 goals in 34 games. Guingamp finished seventh overall in the division, its best ever, and Drogba's stock in France rose significantly as more teams wanted to sign the large striker. Marseilles won the rights to Drogba, and he was more than willing to go because he wanted to prove himself with a top-level team.

Marseilles was made for Drogba. The team had not been at the top of its division for several years but had recently filled the squad with players who promised to make the team the championship contenders they once were. Drogba, now happy in the sun- and fun-filled Mediterranean city, won the hearts of the Marseilles fans when, after each goal he scored, he celebrated with an ever-changing repertoire of dance moves. He finished the season with career high 19 goals in 35 games and helped Marseilles back to the top with a UEFA Cup finals appearance, only to lose in a heart-breaker to Valencia.

Despite the heroic season with Marseilles, when management got word that Chelsea was interested in the striker and was offering $45 million for his contract, they jumped at the offer. Drogba, who was hoping to stay in Marseilles and continue with a team that he figured was moving up in the ranks, was disappointed at having to leave his new team. But Chelsea offered many new possibilities for the 26-year-old. Chelsea had a new owner willing to spend the money to establish a winning team and a new coach in Jose Mourinho, who actively sought out the services of Drogba to help Chelsea's offense.

"I am very happy to be here and am looking forward to playing for my new team," said Drogba. "It is a big chance for me to come here and work with the coach and to play for my new team."

With Drogba on the team, Chelsea bettered its record from the previous year and won the Premiership title with relative ease. Drogba figured prominently in Mourinho's system and was often on the end of many long passes, using his strength and balance to get past the one or two defenders left behind. Chelsea came close to making the

Champions League final that year but was taken out by rivals Liverpool in the semifinals.

Internationally, Drogba has been the center of the Ivorian national team since he began playing with them on a regular basis, but the team's reliance on Drogba has also been its downfall in recent games. It didn't take other teams long to realize that Drogba was their franchise player and to attach two and sometimes three players to dog him through the entire game. African nations tend to play a more open attacking style of play, perfectly suited for the offensive talent of Drogba, but openness often leads to defensive breakdowns and the Ivory Coast has not been immune to such mishaps. While they are still one of the better African teams, the Ivorians still have not yet reached the level of Nigeria or Cameroon, who have made leaps and bounds with their soccer program since the 1990s.

In recent qualifying rounds for the FIFA 2006 World Cup, the Ivory Coast had a few victories against some the weaker teams in its group but failed to challenge the stronger teams. In a qualifying match against rival Cameroon, the Ivory Coast lost 3–2, seriously hurting its chances at making it into the final rounds of the World Cup. Drogba, who scored two goals in the match, threatened to quit playing for Ivory Coast after fans made several threats against the players for losing the match.

Losing Drogba would mean a difficult road to the World Cup for the Ivory Coast.

"If such events should occur (again), I would no longer take the risk to come and play for the national team," said Drogba.

Things suddenly took a dramatic turn for the better when Cameroon failed to beat Egypt in a qualifying match and was eliminated from the tournament, allowing the Ivory Coast its first ever trip to the World Cup.

While Drogba's hopes for his country's success internationally have been renewed, on the club level, Chelsea continues to dominate the English Premier League. Drogba has brought success to each team he has played for and, if things continue to go well for the Ivorian national, then he is well on his way to becoming a legend in his own right.

───────────── SOUTH KOREA ─────────────
Park Ji-Sung
Speed in the Midfield

Not known for producing top-quality soccer stars, South Korea has seen something of a renaissance with the rise of several young players who first grabbed the world's attention during their miraculous run in the 2002 World Cup held in their home country and in Japan.

One of the recent major talents to come from South Korea and make an impact on the European soccer world has been the swift-footed Manchester United midfielder Park Ji-Sung.

He became known to the world at large when he scored a key goal in the 2002 World Cup against Portugal, a goal that eliminated the strong Portuguese side and propelled the Korean team into the elimination rounds, where they shocked the world by beating favorites Italy and Spain before losing to Germany 1–0 in the semifinals.

Soon after the World Cup, teams from around the world began knocking on Ji-Sung's door.

Eventually Ji-Sung chose to sign with Dutch club PSV Eindhoven. Ji-Sung knew that if he could prove himself in the slightly smaller Dutch market, then he could go to any team in Europe and earn a spot with some of the stronger teams.

Ji-Sung's days with PSV were limited, however. Having played in 64 games and scoring 14 goals, he felt he needed to move to a team that could use his natural speed through the midfield. For most games, he was often coming off the bench cold and didn't feel as if he figured into the long-term plans of PSV management. Even after his amazing displays in the Champions League finals, playing excellent defensive soccer and, on occasion, leading rushes down the field and earning assists on goals, he still didn't feel as if he had an assured place on the team. His salvation came in early 2005 when Manchester United coach Sir Alex Ferguson expressed interest in the 24-year-old midfielder. Ferguson wanted to shore up his midfield with younger players because Roy Keane and Ryan Giggs were getting older. Ferguson feared Manchester might not have a proper response to opposition attacks if either were to be injured. Ji-Sung was elated at the chance to prove himself with one of the most respected teams in the soccer world. He happily signed on with Manchester, joining the increasingly youthful squad alongside Cristiano Ronaldo and Wayne Rooney.

"This is just the beginning," said Ji-Sung at the Manchester press conference. "I'm leaving Holland with the confidence that I can do a great job for Manchester United."

With Manchester United, Ji-Sung has proven to be a quality asset in their arsenal of skilled players. Often, veteran Ryan Giggs waits on the sidelines while Ji-Sung tears up the midfield feeding quality passes to Rooney or Van Nistelrooy. Ji-Sung has proven that he can score goals as well. His natural speed allows him to get around defenders, often forcing them to pull him down in frustration after he passes them, leading to free-kick opportunities almost every game. The only problem for Ji-Sung in the highly competitive English Premier League is that if he doesn't produce results on a regular basis, his place on the team is not assured. But Ji-Sung has never been one to back down from a challenge.

CZECH REPUBLIC
Pavel Nedved
Extreme Work Ethic

Watching the golden-haired Czech player on the field, one thing stands out above all his talents: the man never stops moving. Whether he is on the ball attacking or defending, Pavel Nedved seems to have an internal engine that allows him continually to be on the move. Not only does he have one of the most energetic attitudes in the game today, he is also regarded as one of the best playmakers. All these accolades for a boy who was almost steered into the accounting profession by his parents because they thought he could make better money putting numbers on a balance sheet than on a score sheet. Luckily, he chose the latter.

When he began his career with Czech team Dukla Praga at the age of 19, Nedved enjoyed instant success and was moved to the larger, more popular Sparta Prague team, where his contribution to the team paid off with three consecutive league titles between 1992 and 1995.

After the Czech Republic's surprising run to the finals of the European Cup in 1996, Nedved quickly caught the attention of Italian team Lazio and was promptly signed for the start of the 1996–97 season. His success showed a marked difference from the criticism he received at the beginning of his career.

"Pavel Nedved will never be a big player. He should be happy sitting on the bench at Sparta," said his former Sparta coach, who would later eat his words as the speedy midfielder led his team to several championships.

With Lazio, Nedved's talents came to the fore. Scoring 11 goals in his first season and setting up many others, Lazio's position in the Serie A league started to climb and, by his second year with the team, they won the Coppa Italia. The year after that, Lazio won the 1999 European Cup Winners Cup.

After leading his team to the Italian league title in 2000, Nedved wanted to find a team that had a chance at winning the Champions League title, something every soccer player dreams of, and he ended up signing with Lazio rivals, Juventus.

Nedved was a welcome addition to the Juve squad, which had just lost midfield superstar Zinedine Zidane to Real Madrid. The loss of Zidane left a large hole in the Juve midfield, but Nedved quickly sprinted his way into the hearts of the fans and the Juventus playbook. After a few shaky games, Nedved adjusted to the Juventus style of play and sprinted all over the field, playing up to the high expectations set for him.

In 2003, Nedved got his wish of making it far into Champions League play with a stellar performance against Real Madrid in the semifinals, scoring the third goal in the second leg of the semis. The win took them through to the finals, but Nedved picked up a yellow card and was automatically taken out of the final match against Serie A rivals AC Milan. Without the help of Nedved on penalties, Juventus eventually lost the game.

"It was an awful feeling," said Nedved after the game. "It was my dream to win the Champions League, and I felt I would never have a better chance than with Juventus."

Despite the loss in the Champions League, Nedved was awarded the highly treasured Ballon D'or award that goes to the best player in European soccer. He is not a player like Ronaldinho or Cristiano Ronaldo, who are known for their dribbling skills and almost magical skills, but his work ethic is like none other in the European leagues. Through sheer speed, tenacity and vision, Nedved is an indispensable part of any team. He is able to score goals with equal power from both the left and right foot, and his ability to place a precise shot in the penalty area for the striker makes him one of the best assets on any team. When he was taken out of the semifinals against Greece in the 2004 Euro Cup on a red card, the Czech team lost their most valuable player and was eventually eliminated from the tournament.

At 33, the Czech superstar shows no signs of slowing down and enters the 2005–06 season hoping to take Juventus to the Serie A title and, hopefully, to the Champions league finals once again.

"All I try and do is play better every time I walk on to the pitch. I work hard on the training ground because I always believe there is more to come from me," said Nedved.

―――――――――――――― UKRAINE ――――――――――――――

Andriy Shevchenko
Lethal Weapon

With over 100 goals in his six seasons with AC Milan, Andriy Shevchenko, in the famously defensive-minded Italian League, has become one of the most prolific goal scorers in European soccer.

Born in the town of Dvirkivshchyna just a few miles away from Chernobyl, Shevchenko got off to a rough start in life. In 1986, at just nine years old, he was forced to leave his hometown when the nuclear power plant in Chernobyl exploded, sending toxic radiation for miles in all directions. After relocating to a new town, Shevchenko got his first break in soccer at the age of 14 when he was spotted by a scout from Dynamo Kiev, who knew that the kid needed work but saw that he had an instinct for scoring goals. After a few years on the junior team refining his skills and putting on some muscle, Shevchenko got his first call up to the professional level at the age of 17 and put his early setbacks far behind him.

Shevchenko or "Sheva," as he is more widely known, began his career with Ukrainian club Dynamo Kiev in 1994. Although he only appeared in 16 matches, scoring one goal in his first year, his second year with the club saw a marked improvement when he had16 goals in 31 matches. His talent for pure goal scoring was evident from the beginning of his career.

Sheva's lighting quick runs and skilled dribbling on the ball make a hard target for any defender to follow. When matched with a good set-up man in the midfield position, Sheva is even more deadly inside the penalty area. He is the definition of what a striker should be. When he has the ball, his only thought is to put it past the goalkeeper. His single-mindedness has earned him an enviable reputation on the field.

"When a striker has the ball, he must think of nothing but scoring. It's got nothing to do with egotism; it's just doing his job. My sole aim is to score goals, not for myself, but for the team," Shevchenko explained in an interview with FIFA.com.

With Dynamo Kiev, Shevchenko, under the guidance of Valeri Lobanovsky, flourished into one of the team's most prominent and skillful players. The highlight of his career with Dynamo came in the 1997–98 campaign for the Champions League title against Barcelona. In the group qualifying rounds, Barcelona was the clear favorite; few in the soccer world gave Dynamo Kiev a chance of beating the Spanish powerhouse. Barcelona, however, did not figure on the talents of Shevchenko, who led his team to a 3–0 victory in the first match and scored a hat trick in the second match, which Dynamo also won 4–0. Barcelona fans could hardly believe that their team was beaten by a group of relative unknowns and taken out of the elimination rounds. Unfortunately, Dynamo was easily beaten by Juventus in the quarterfinals 5-2 and was eliminated from the Champions League. But Shevchenko had made his mark.

His aggressive attacking style and quickness on the ball caught the attention of many teams seeking a pure goal-scoring striker. Shevchenko had accumulated five league titles and two national cups with Dynamo and had scored 77 goals in all. As with all quality players languishing in the smaller markets, Shevchenko needed to move to the more skilled European leagues to bring his game to higher level and become the kind of player he had worshiped as a kid. He soon found a home with Italian Serie A powerhouse, AC Milan.

"Shevchenko is the best attacker in Europe. He has a great deal of consistency and he just keeps scoring—which in Italian football is very difficult," said his current coach Carlo Ancelotti. "He is a complete player, someone who can do everything on a football field."

In his first season with the club, Sheva scored a career high of 24 goals, won the Serie A scoring title and became a favorite in Milan to fans who were not used to strikers scoring so many goals. He equaled his career-high goal numbers again in the next season.

His most memorable year came in 2003 in the Champions league final against Italian Serie A rivals Juventus. It had been a long hard fought battle because AC Milan had to dispose of difficult opponents along the way, but with the help of veterans like Paolo Maldini and young strikers like Shevchenko, Milan always came out victorious. The final would be revenge for Shevchenko because Juventus eliminated his old team Dynamo Kiev in the 1998 Champions League quarterfinals. This time, however, Shevchenko had the players alongside him that could beat Juventus.

Italian soccer is well known for being overly defensive, and the final between Juventus and Milan was no exception. Both teams had their chances during regulation time but couldn't put anything on the scoreboard. Still undecided after extra time, both coaches readied their list of players to lineup for a penalty shot. After both teams traded goals, the shoot out was tied as Shevchenko stepped up to the penalty area. AC Milan fans held their breath as Shevchenko began his run and, with a simple yet decisive kick, he won the game for Milan.

"I will never forget scoring that goal," said Shevchenko, the first ever Ukranian player to win the Champions League title.

The good news didn't stop there for the talented striker. He added more trophies to his long list when he won the scoring title again in the Serie A league and received the 2004 Golden Ball Award given to the top European player of the year.

"I'm Ukrainian and proud of it. I would like to thank all the people who have helped me win it, and I would like to dedicate the Golden Ball to the people of Ukraine," said Shevchenko at the awards gala.

Shevchenko found himself in the same position as the 2003 Champions League finals when AC Milan played against Liverpool in the 2005 edition. After mowing their way through the competition in the qualifying rounds, AC Milan was the heavy favorite in the final against Liverpool, who was seen as lucky to be in the final given their fifth-place finish in the English Premiership.

Milan took the lead early in the game on a goal from Captain Paolo Maldini at just one minute into the first half. Milan had possession of the ball for most of the first half, running circles around the Liverpool players, who looked outclassed in every way. When Hernan Crespo scored the second and third goals at the 39th and 44th minute of the half, all seemed to be lost for Liverpool. But as quickly as Milan scored its goals, Liverpool came back with a little skill and a little luck with goals from Steven Gerrard, Vladimir Smicer and Xabi Alonso. No one broke the tie during regulation and extra time, and the two teams were forced to decide the championship on penalty shots.

Milan's lineup for the penalty shootout was Serginho, Andrea Pirlo, Jon Tomasson, Kaka, and finally, Shevchenko. After trading goals and saves, Shevchenko was left to tie up the penalties. Sheva took his place at the penalty marker. Liverpool goaltender Jerzy Dudek bounced from side to side, ready to pounce on the ball. Shevchenko approached the ball and kicked it toward the left-hand corner. Dudek, guessing the right direction of the shot, made the initial save, but the ball bounced back directly onto Shevchenko's foot. He tried to put the ball into the open net, but Dudek made an incredible, desperate save that sent the ball up and over the net. As the Liverpool players swarmed their heroic goaltender, Shevchenko lowered his head in disbelief at missing the shot.

"I was sure I could score from a yard. I could have taken that shot 10,000 times and scored," said a distraught Shevchenko after the game. "If that had gone in, with a minute left, it would have been the end."

After the defeat in the Champions League final, Shevchenko wanted to relax over the summer at his villa in the picturesque city of Lake Como in Northern Italy, but he was hounded by media speculation and rumors that he was set to move to Chelsea. Owner Roman Abramovich reportedly offered the outrageous sum of $98 million and striker Hernan Crespo in return for Shevchenko. The rumors intensified after Italian television cameras caught Shevchenko and Milan coach Carlo Ancelotti in an argument where Shevchenko allegedly said that if Ancelotti was unhappy with his performance, then he would leave. Both coach and player were quick to deny the trade rumors.

"If Milan wanted to sell me, I wouldn't leave. I have no intention of leaving this club. Milan wants me, and I want Milan; that is enough for me," said Shevchenko.

"Shevchenko remains a key figure for Milan. I can assure you he will stay at Milan and I don't think there were any doubts," said Ancelotti, reassuring the public that Shevchenko was worth more to him on the team than any amount of money offered. "It was simply a normal argument between a coach and a player."

Despite the occasional setback, things continue to go well for Shevchenko with AC Milan. He is partnered with some of the best players in the game, and his own skill on the field continues to improve. The only obstacle standing in his way is victory on an international stage.

On the national side, things haven't been as successful, but Shevchenko has fond memories of playing for his country and is positive about the future of the Ukrainian team. While he doesn't have the level of players beside him that he does with Milan, the talent coming from the Ukrainian leagues is providing some exciting soccer.

"I dream of success with Ukraine,' said Shevchenko, hoping to carry his successes on the club level into the international arena. The mark of a true superstar in soccer has always been to win in the major international events like the Euro Cup and World Cup.

In an interview with the *Guardian*, Ukrainian coach Oleg Blokhin stated just how important Sheva is to the success of the national team: "Andriy is our locomotive. We don't have players of the caliber of Kaka, Cafu and Maldini to play alongside him, but he carries the team up."

The race to the 2006 World Cup is looking positive for the Ukrainian side. They are in first place with 24 points, ahead of other veteran World Cup countries in their grouping like Turkey, Greece and Denmark. It will be a challenge for them to move far into the tournament, but there is always a chance with Shevchenko leading the team through the stages.

──────────── CANADA ────────────

Owen Hargreaves
The Best They've Got

Canada has never been known as a soccer nation. Hockey dominates the hearts and minds of most Canadian children growing up, given its long, successful history of producing the best hockey players in the world. But little by little, soccer is making inroads into the great white north, and several players have risen from the relative obscurity of the fledgling United Soccer League to the more lucrative European leagues. The most famous of these has been Owen Hargreaves.

Hargreaves got his start playing on the soccer fields of Calgary, Alberta. Although soccer wasn't normally the sport of choice for a young Canadian boy, Hargreaves chose to stay in the local program rather than join the rest of his friends playing street hockey. Although he took part in the occasional hockey game, soccer was his passion. It wasn't long before Hargreaves' talent was noticed by a German scout, who recognized that he was too good to be languishing in the Canadian soccer leagues and moved the 16-year-old to Germany to train with Bayern Munich and to play on its reserve side. The move was a major opportunity for the young Canadian, but he didn't get his chance to prove himself for several years, watching most of Bayern's games from the sidelines.

His golden opportunity came when team regular Stefan Effenberg was suspended in Champions League play and Hargreaves replaced him. His performance during the 2001 Champions league season proved so successful for Bayern that he soon found himself in most games on the first team, and he hasn't looked back. He's been a regular in the Bayern midfield helping the team make it all the way to the final of the Champions League, where they faced off against Valencia. He was put on the field to stymie the speedy Valencia attackers and, with the help of his teammates, kept a tight defensive flow to the game. No winner emerged during regulation time or in extra time, so it was down to penalty shootouts to decide the Champions winner. When it came time for the shootouts, Hargreaves scored to help Bayern take the Champions League title on penalties 5–4.

"I wasn't really nervous at all," said Hargreaves in a *Champions* magazine interview. "I was more excited and anxious just to get it going because your whole life you wait for an opportunity like that."

On the international level, although he was born and raised in Canada, Hargreaves decided to play for the England national team because his parents were of English and Welsh descent. Playing for Canada was also an option, but Canada has never qualified for any major international tournaments, and Hargreaves wanted to play for a team that had a chance at winning.

As he gears up for another season with Bayern Munich, Hargreaves has made it known that he is looking for an English Premier club to buy out his contract. No offers have come yet, but any team that needs an excellent defensive midfielder would be lucky to pick him up. He wants to continue to play for England and would like to live there as well, but he will always be a Canadian at heart.

Freddy Adu
America's Soccer Prodigy

Born in Ghana, Freddy Adu immigrated to the United States when he was just eight years old when his mother, Emelia, won a green card lottery. The decision forever changed his life. He had already shown interest in soccer from an early age but never had the benefits of coaching. Freddy had his lessons on a dirt- and sand-covered field, often with men twice his age. They treated him just like one of the other players once they saw that Freddy could run circles around many of the players. He attributes these hard lessons on the field to giving him the will and strength to take on any opponent no matter what size.

"It was awesome," explained Adu of his time growing up in Ghana, "because, you know, like, there was no coaches, no one to tell you what to do. It was just, you play and learn stuff on your own."

When he came to the United States, the U.S. Olympic Development Program quickly noticed his skills when he was just nine years old, and he was shipped off to the youth trials at the national soccer camp. He impressed the coaches there enough for them to place Freddy in a series of youth-squad games against countries like Italy.

After seeing Adu play, many European league teams such as Manchester United and Inter Milan wanted to sign Adu to their junior programs. But Adu's mother refused because she wanted him to be close to home and to have access to an American education. Instead, Freddy opted to sign with the Major League Soccer's (MLS) D.C United in 2003.

Adu also began to play on the international level that year in the FIFA Under-17 World Cup and the World Youth Championships. His performances in the two tournaments had sports media around the United States following the young phenom's every move. He helped the U.S. National Team qualify for the FIFA U-17 World Cup with a goal and an assist, defeating Jamaica 3–0. Playing against South Korea, Adu scored a hat trick, sealing the victory. He scored another goal in a game against Sierra Leone in the final minutes to put the U.S. into the quarterfinals against Brazil. Unfortunately, the U.S. lost to the eventual champions, but Adu's mark on the world stage had been set. Adu had become hot property and, not missing out on the marketability of young talent, Nike quickly jumped on the band-wagon and signed him to a $1-million endorse-ment deal. All this and the boy was just 14 years old. More and more it looked like Freddy's mother had made the right decision turning down the offers from the large European teams.

"I just love it so much, you know," Adu said, using his best American teenager vocabulary in an interview with CBS. "When I'm out there on the field, I'm in a whole different world, you know? It's like I'm just having so much fun."

Even the likes of Pele chimed in on the skills of the young American when they were filming a Pepsi commercial. "I told him, 'Listen. God give you, you know, the gift to play football.'"

With all the attention that has been on the young star, he has also garnered his fair share of criticism from those who think he is too young to play soccer professionally. Although he has shown a great deal of potential, he only scored five goals in 30 matches and was often heard in the media complaining about the amount of time he was on the field. Many have suggested that Adu needs more time to develop with players his own age, not just physically but mentally. Throwing a kid in to play against men can harm his development as a soccer player and ruin his chances of future success. Some detractors have even said that Freddy's mother altered his Ghanian birth certificate and that he is actually older than the 15 years he claims.

Despite the controversy that surrounds Adu, he remains focused on playing soccer and developing into a player with skill, strength and finesse like his idols Pele and Maradona.

Despite his critics and his worshipers, Adu only has to worry about one person's opinion—his coach, Bruce Arena. "He's a very graceful athlete," said Arena. "His first touch and his vision are outstanding for a player of his age."

Notes on Sources

Since all of the players in this book are still playing the game today, most information has come from magazine articles, internet sources and a few newspapers that find their way to North American shores from the mainly European sports writers dedicated to following soccer.

BBC. Various entries. www.bbc.co.uk.

Bellos, Alex. *Futebol: The Brazilian way of Life.* London: Bloomsbury Press, 2003.

Beckham, David. *Beckham: Both Feet on the Ground: An Autobiography.* New York: Harper Collins, 2003.

Buffon Online: A Site Dedicated to Gigi Buffon. www.buffononline.com.

Didier Drogba. Official Website. www.didierdrogba.com.

FIFA: The Official Website of the Fédération Internationale de Football Association. www.fifa.com.

Freddy Adu: Official Website. www.freddyadu.com.

One United: Manchester United Official Website. www.manutd.com.

Philippe, Jean. *Zidane: Le Roi Modeste.* Paris: L'Archipel, 2002.

Radnedge, Keir. *The Complete Encyclopedia of Soccer.* London: Carlton Books, 2004.

Real Madrid C.F. Web Official / Real Madrid C.F. Official Web. www.realmadrid.com.

Sky Sports: The Best Sport Coverage From Around the World. www.skysports.com.

The Times. www.timesonline.co.uk.

World Cup Soccer and Global Football Information: Soccerphile. www.soccerphile.com.

UEFA.com: Europe's Football Website. www.UEFA.com.

Various magazine articles from imported British and European publications published in 2004 and 2005—*Champions, FourFourTwo, Soccer Digest, Soccer Italia, Striker* and *World Soccer.*

J. Alexander Poulton

J.Alexander Poulton is a writer, reader and lover of the world's most popular sport. His interest in soccer came relatively late in life, having grown up in hockey-mad Montreal, Canada. He became a lifetime fan of the game after watching the 1990 World Cup when underdog Cameroon surprised the world making it all the way to the quarter finals before losing in extra time to the English. Since then he has been a faithful devotee of soccer (football to the rest of the world).

He earned his BA in English Literature from McGill University and his graduate diploma in Journalism from Concordia University.

OverTime Books

If you enjoyed
WORLD'S GREATEST SOCCER PLAYERS
be sure to check out these other great titles
from OverTime Books:

COMING SEPTEMBER 2006

GREATEST STANLEY CUP VICTORIES
by J. Alexander Poulton
A look back at some of the NHL's most memorable battles for hockey supremacy.
$9.95 • ISBN10 1-897277-06-7 • ISBN13 978-1897277-06-5 • 5.25" x 8.25" • 144 pages

HOCKEY'S HOTTEST PLAYERS:
The On-and Off-Ice Stories of the Superstars
by Arpon Basu
Sports journalist Arpon Basu profiles today's rising stars in the National Hockey League. He looks not only at their on-ice performance and statistics but also probes the human story behind their victories and struggles, revealing the journey they've taken to reach the highest echelons of their sport.
$9.95 • ISBN10 0-9737681-3-4 • ISBN13 978-0-9737681-3-8 • 5.25" x 8.25" • 144 pages

NEW SEPTEMBER 2006

CANADIAN HOCKEY TRIVIA
by J. Alexander Poulton
Hockey is so much a part of Canadian life that the theme song to Hockey Night in Canada has been called our unofficial national anthem. Read the fascinating facts from Canada's favorite game such as the almost-forgotten Winnipeg Falcons, who were the first Canadian team to win Olympic gold in 1920 and Dennis O'Brien, who holds the record for most NHL teams played for in a single season.
$9.95 • ISBN10 1-897277-01-6 • ISBN13 978-1-897277-01-0 • 5.25" x 8.25" • 144 pages

NEW SEPTEMBER 2006

THE EDMONTON OILERS
by Peter Boer
A fascinating account of the Cinderella team from the Canadian prairies that became an NHL dynasty and spawned some of the league's greatest stars: Wayne Gretzky, Mark Messier, Paul Coffey and Grant Fuhr among them.
$9.95 • ISBN10: 1-897277-02-4 • ISBN13: 978-1-897277-02-7 • 5.25" x 8.25" • 144 pages

EXTREME SNOWBOARDING: Canada's Best Riders
by Tom Peacock
Canada's best snowboarders take the rides of their lives, attacking impossible moundainnsides, launching giant cliffs and busting insane jumps. Read stories of extreme snowboarding from Victoria Jealouse, Kevin Sansalone, Shin Campos, Ross Rebagliati and more.
$9.95 • ISBN10: 0-9737681-1-8 • ISBN13: 978-0-9737681-1-4 • 5.25" x 8.25" • 144 pages

Lone Pine Publishing is the exclusive distributor for OverTime Books.
If you cannot find these titles at your local bookstore, contact us:

Canada: 1-800-661-9017   USA: 1-800-518-3541